Takeo Doi graduated from the University of Tokyo in 1942. He has held a number of posts at American institutes and universities, including the Menninger School of Psychiatry and the San Francisco Psychoanalytic Institute, and was visiting scientist at the National Institute of Mental Health, Bethesda, Maryland. He headed the psychiatric department at St. Luke's International Hospital in Tokyo for a number of years, and was also a professor in the schools of Health Science and Medicine at the University of Tokyo, and a professor at International Christian University. He now serves as a consultant to St. Luke's and is also a visiting scholar at the PHP Research Institute in Tokyo. Dr. Doi has published a number of works, including the Japanese bestseller *Amae no Kōzō* (*The Anatomy of Dependence*, Kodansha International) and *The Psychological World of Natsume Soseki* (Harvard University Press). *Omote to ura*, of which *The Anatomy of Self* is a translation, was published by Kōbundō in March, 1985, and is another bestseller in Japan.

Mark A. Harbison is a doctoral candidate in Japanese literature at Stanford University. Currently based in Tokyo, his translations include Konishi Jinichi's *A History of Japanese Literature* (Princeton University Press) and many books on art, pop-art, literature, and social criticism. He has published translations of short stories by Nagai Kafu, Abe Akira, Furui Yoshikichi, and Nakagami Kenji. His translation of Oe Kenzaburo's *Rouze up, O, Young Men of the New Age* (*Atarashii Hito yo! Mezameyo*) will be published by Kodansha International.

Edward T. Hall is a distinguished anthropologist, educator, and author. He received his Ph.D. from Columbia University in 1942. Prof. Hall has held numerous posts and engaged in extensive research in anthropology. He was professor of anthropology at Northwestern University from 1967-1977 and now heads his own research institute in New Mexico. A prolific writer, Prof. Hall is the author of *The Silent Language*, *The Hidden Dimension*, *The Fourth Dimension in Architecture*, *Beyond Culture*, *The Dance of Life*, and *Hidden Differences*.

THE ANATOMY OF SELF

The Individual Versus Society

Takeo Doi, M.D.

Translated by Mark A. Harbison

Foreword by Edward Hall

KODANSHA INTERNATIONAL
Tokyo • New York • London

Acknowledgments and credits: citation on p. 19, *Pensées* by Blaise Pascal, tr. by A. J. Krailsheimer (Middlesex, Penguin Books, 1984), reprinted by permission of Penguin Books, Ltd.; p. 47, *The Theory of Social and Economic Organization* by Max Weber, tr. by A. M. Henderson and Talcott Parsons, and ed. by Talcott Parsons, copyright 1947, renewed 1975 by Talcott Parsons, reprinted by permission of the publisher, The Free Press, a division of Macmillan, Inc.; p. 53, *Language, Thought and Reality: Selected Writings of Benjamin Lee Whorf* (Boston: Massachusetts Institute of Technology, 1965), by permission; p. 83, *Language and Silence* by George Steiner (New York: Atheneum, 1967); p. 88, *The Principles of Psychology* by William James (New York: Dover Publications, 1950), by permission; p. 96, *Ego Psychology and the Problem of Adaptation* by Heinz Hartmann (New York: International Universities Press, 1961); p. 98, *The Standard Edition of the Complete Psychological Works of Sigmund Freud*, tr. and ed. by Richard Strachey (London: The Hogarth Press, 1971), by permission of Sigmund Freud Copyrights Ltd., The Institute of Psycho-Analysis, and The Hogarth Press; p. 99, *Hitler in Ourselves* by Max Picard, tr. by Heinrich Hauser (Hinsdale, Illinois: Henry Regnery Co., 1947); pp. 101–102, *Nineteen Eighty-Four* by George Orwell (Middlesex, Penguin Books, 1984), reprinted by permission of Penguin Books, Ltd.; p. 112, *Beyond Good and Evil* by Friedrich Nietzsche, tr. by R. J. Hollingdale (Middlesex, Penguin Books, 1984), reprinted by permission of Penguin Books, Ltd.; *The Life and Work of Sigmund Freud* by Ernest Jones (New York: Basic Books, 1953); p. 144, *Faust* by Johann Wolfgang Goethe, tr. by Philip Wayne (Middlesex, Penguin Books, 1985), reprinted by permission of Penguin Books, Ltd.; p. 149, *Goethe: Poems and Epigrams* by Johann Wolfgang Von Goethe, selected, translated and with an introduction by Michael Hamburger (London: The Anvil Press, 1983), by permission; pp. 157–163, *Omote and Ura: Concepts Derived from the Japanese 2-Fold Structure of Consciousness* by Takeo Doi (Baltimore: Williams and Wilkins, 1973). Biblical quotations are from *The New English Bible New Testament*, 2nd edition, (Cambridge: Cambridge University Press, 1970), by permission of Oxford and Cambridge University Presses. Citations of Shakespeare's plays are from *The Complete Works of William Shakespeare*, ed. by Peter Alexander (London and Glasgow: William Collins, Sons and Company Limited, 1985), by permission.

Originally published under the title *Omote to ura* by Kōbundō, 1985.

Distributed in the United States by Kodansha America, Inc., 114 Fifth Avenue, New York, N.Y. 10011, and in the United Kingdom and continental Europe by Kodansha Europe Ltd., Gillingham House, 38-44 Gillingham Street, London SW1V 1HU. Published by Kodansha International Ltd., 17-14 Otowa 1-chome, Bunkyo-ku, Tokyo 112, and Kodansha America, Inc. All rights reserved. Printed in Japan.

First English edition, 1986   LCC 85-23931
First paperback edition, 1988   ISBN 0-87011-902-8
91 92 93 10 9 8 7 6 5 4 3   ISBN 4-7700-1402-3 (in Japan)

CONTENTS

Foreword

It is a great privilege for me to be able to introduce *The Anatomy of Self*. When Dr. Doi asked me to write this modest preface I couldn't help but anticipate the pleasure and the honor accorded me. I was not prepared—even though I was familiar with, in fact have always been deeply interested in, Dr. Doi's studies—for the excitement I would experience on reading this new book. It brought home to me once again the absolute obligation that each of us has—in spite of the risks—to share our insights with others and the great loss when people lack the confidence, energy, or courage to describe systematically the conceptual worlds in which they live.

Dr. Doi's volume concerns a subject which has never been far from my heart: the study of men's minds and the relationship of human extensions to those minds. That is what, in a more restricted sense, is known as the Sapir-Whorf hypothesis, or the study of the relation of language to thought as a scientific tool. To describe this book would, since it sparks so many ideas in the reader, require more space than the book itself. I must be content therefore with saying that Dr. Doi's analysis is multi-level and that his insights will be stimulating scholars long after both of us are dead.

Since Dr. Doi's *Introduction* informs the reader as to the

direction and contents of this extraordinary volume, I have chosen to define my role as that of concentrating—in so far as is possible in a few words—on the significance of the concepts set forth in *The Anatomy of Self* when viewed in the context of the working *interface* of the Japanese and American cultures. That is, I have set as my task a discussion of a few of the implications for the disciplines concerned with the study of human behavior as well for intercultural understanding of the concepts of *tatemae* and *honne* and *omote* and *ura* as described by Dr. Doi. As it turns out they are not inconsiderable and, as is frequently the case, small, apparently inconsequential events can—when properly understood—have deep implications for our understanding of the basics of human relations.

It is both interesting and relevant that on the very day that I received the manuscript for *The Anatomy of Self* (the Japanese title is *Omote to Ura*) I had been reading the work of another psychiatrist, Erich Fromm's *The Anatomy of Human Destructiveness*. Both authors begin by explaining that the task they had set themselves was much greater than anticipated, that they were deeply involved in their subject and that they found it necessary to *go beyond the boundaries of their disciplines and to explore other fields*. I myself had had a parallel experience in the 1940s when I found it necessary to report on (thanks to Dr. Doi) the *tatemae* and the *ura* of public officials in Denver regarding the chances of instituting what was later known as "Equal Opportunity" in employment. In those days there were no models with accompanying terminology for the difference between people's public statements and their private views which were nevertheless guiding policy. My point was that, given my own mission of ascertaining attitudes concerning "equal opportunity," I knew that the very mention of such an idea—viewed from the perspective of the climate of the times—would be simply to elicit the cliched statements of *tatemae* (the public ideal) without considering the operational reality that is the other side of the coin. In order to get at *honne* (where the individual was coming from) it was necessary to go beyond the normal realms of social science and public opinion research and find a suitable model which might explain what was being observed during my interviews. Since I knew that I would get (on the verbal level) only what I was supposed to hear, I directed my attention to the nonverbal responses of my respondents, such as waiting times in the reception areas of offices, how interruptions were received (as welcome or not), and the like. The only model I was familiar with at that time that fit what I had been observing in the course of the interviews was Freudian. The title of my paper was "The Freudian Error as an Aid in Determining Attitudes." I was naive enough then to assume that the goal of public opinion research was the determination of *real* attitudes, and that I was making a contribution to public opinion research by adding a new dimension to that field. As might have been predicted, my paper was turned down by the leading public opinion journals in the United States and was finally published in the *International Journal of Opinion and Attitude Research* (Vol. 3, No. 1, 1949).

The point, I now realize, thanks to Dr. Doi's insights, is that in the United States it is permissible to describe the conventions and verbal expressions of *tatemae*, but one's analysis must *not* link the *tatemae* of the situation with *honne*—what is taking place behind the mask presented to the public. In Japan, however, the two are irrevocably linked in people's minds—one cannot consider the outside independently of the inside, the front door from the back door, face independently of mind, which leads to Dr. Doi's construction of his "two-fold theory of consciousness for the Japanese." In the West we know about *honne*, which deals with people's true motives, but we must pretend that it does not exist; when *honne* is discussed there is the accompanying feeling that there is something dirty involved simply in bringing up the subject.

The Anatomy of Self therefore sheds additional light on American attitudes toward Freud, psychology in general, and sex. These same attitudes are found even among practitioners of social science and may explain some of their dependence on questionnaires probing people's publicly-held thoughts at the expense of deeper, more penetrating but also more subjective studies. In fact, according to some very well-known practitioners of the field, even making observations of people's natural behavior in public in order to get at the underlying patterns—without first getting their written consent—is considered *wrong*. There is, according to the popes of the field, no way of studying the "tacit" dimensions of culture, because as soon as the question is raised what occurs is somewhat like being on camera and being told to act naturally. This attitude blocks from scientific examination the very features of culture and leads to the greatest misunderstandings when the representatives of different cultures meet. What we can assume from this is that the private or personal side of life is viewed as inevitably in opposition to the public good. That is, in the West, *tatemae* is forever alienated from *honne*, whereas in Japan the two are linked and the non-word dimensions of culture are taken for real. As they should be.

For anyone wishing to gain fresh insights into the relationship between the study of psychology and culture, the relationship between language and mind, as well as that between the Americans and the Japanese, this book can only be considered required reading. Dr. Doi has done us all a great favor in writing it.

Edward T. Hall
Emeritus Professor of Anthropology
Northwestern University

Preface

Let me begin by saying a word about the nature of this book. As its title suggests, this book attempts to grasp human phenomena in general from the perspective of *omote* and *ura*, two concepts representing a way of looking at things that is unique to the Japanese language. As we shall see, it is possible to approximate these terms in English: *Recto-verso*, heads and tails, outside-inside, facade-interior, and so on, all give an impression of the meaning of *omote* and *ura*. Similarly, facade and truth, mask and real face, outward appearance and inner reality all hint at the meaning of *tatemae* and *honne*. But none of these correspondences between the Japanese terms and English is precisely correct. For one thing, the English expressions make of these dyadic pairs hierarchical oppositions: facade (*omote*) versus inner truth (*ura*), outside versus inside, appearance versus reality, and, ultimately, evil versus good. In every case, the term corresponding to *omote* is seen as a negation, as a complication of the more "authentic" half of the pair. While this tendency is certainly not absent in modern Japanese usage of the terms, I felt that forcing them into English would only serve to exacerbate the problem and, therefore, decided to retain the original Japanese words in the English version of my book.

To the extent that *omote* and *ura* are uniquely Japanese, this book has something of the character of the so-called *Nihonjin-ron* (theories of the Japanese). As was true of *Amae no Kōzō* (published in English as *The Anatomy of Dependence*), however, my purpose in writing this book is not merely to offer yet another theory explaining the Japanese. My real aim is to examine these Japanese concepts in light of ideas that originate in the West and, by doing so, to deepen them and to discover in them a universal significance. This has been the direction of my scholarly work from the very beginning.

I have taken this direction because I am a practicing clinical psychiatrist. The specialist's jargon is almost useless in a clinical situation. The whole battle is won or lost depending on what kind of communication the psychiatrist is able to establish with the patient. But precisely because this is true, psychiatrists must always keep their eyes open to what underlies language—the nuances that exist in the depths of words—and they must take responsibility for the words that they use themselves.

Therefore, even though I do discuss the health or illness of the mind, that is not the premise of my argument. Rather, for the reasons stated above, that distinction itself is subjected to analysis. It is for the same reasons that, in my discussion of other issues, I have always attempted first to clarify the meanings of the words I am using. And, again, this is why I am asking my foreign readers to go to the trouble of learning a number of terms in Japanese.

I have been forced to go far beyond the boundaries of my own academic specialty, searching for insights in the fields of sociology, philosophy, literature, and religion. This book is a synthesis of what I have gained from this search, and I hope that the reader will accept it as such. I have wanted to write a book like this for many years, and I am very pleased to have finally finished it, and to see it published.

Included in the English edition are two appendices. The first is from a book I published in 1975, *Amae Zakkō* (Collected Essays on *Amae*), and the second is a paper I published in English in the *Journal of Mental and Nervous Disease* in 1973.

I would like to express my gratitude to the many people involved in the Japanese and English editions. For the English edition, I am indebted to Lisa Oyama and Ichiba Shinji, my editors at Kodansha International. I am very pleased that they have chosen as the title of the English edition *The Anatomy of Self: The Individual versus Society*, for I believe it truly matches what the original Japanese title, *Omote to Ura*, evokes for Japanese readers. My translator, Mark A. Harbison, not only translated the book, but also prepared translations of the Japanese texts I have cited and provided explanatory notes for the Western reader. Translations from Hans Asmussen's *Das Geheimnis der Liebe* are my own. Finally, I would like to thank my friend and colleague Prof. Edward T. Hall, who graciously agreed to write the foreword for my book.

Doi Takeo
December, 1985

Cette duplicité de l'homme est si visible, qu'il y en a qui ont pensé que nous avions deux âmes.

Pascal

Introduction

This book is a sequel to *The Anatomy of Dependence* (*Amae no Kōzō*).[1] But it is a sequel only in the sense that it has taken me this long to return to a subject that I have been interested in for some time. From the very beginning, *omote* and *ura* were central to my theory of dependence (*amae*).

My interest in this subject originated in the strong impression I received from a patient I treated shortly after returning from my first trip to the United States. The patient was reacting violently to the fact that everyone around her, even her mother, had an *omote* and an *ura*. In concluding my report on this patient, I added a note to the effect that the phenomenon of subtle changes in attitude depending on whether a situation was perceived as *omote* or *ura* was a basic mode of behavior among the Japanese, and that alienation was the inevitable result if this fact were challenged.

Subsequently, I discussed this behavior pattern in my article *Seishin Bunseki* (Psychoanalysis, 1956), pointing out that it was an effective means of dealing with ambivalence.[2] In fact, this is precisely the argument that I have now developed in this book, and I still find it surprising at times that the germ of this idea was already in my mind more than thirty years ago, when I was a young psychiatrist just returning from my first trip to the United States after conducting research there.

However, my interest in *omote* and *ura* somehow got put on the back burner at this point, as I became almost completely absorbed in developing my theory of *amae*, and it was not until about ten years ago that my attention turned once again to the problem of *omote* and *ura*. My renewed interest was related to the fact that I had become interested in the possibility of dealing with psychopathology by using the concept of secrets (*himitsu*).

I had been aware of the importance of the concept of secrets for some time, due to the influence of Dr. Rudolph Ekstein, with whom I studied during my first stay in the United States. In fact, in my *Seishin Ryōhō to Seishin Bunseki* (Psychotherapy and Psychoanalysis),[3] first published in 1961, I explained the various methods of psychotherapy and their respective characteristics entirely from the viewpoint of this concept of secrets. It was around the same time that I began to feel, albeit vaguely, that this concept was important not only in considering psychotherapy, but also, more broadly, in getting at the essential nature of psychopathology itself.

My first attempt to go further was a short paper published in 1970, "*Naze seishinka ni tsuite henken o motsu ka?*" (Why Do People Have a Prejudice Against Psychiatry?).[4] The gist of my argument can be summarized as follows. All prejudice arises from the attempt to rationalize anxiety in the face of the unfamiliar, and prejudice against the mentally disturbed also originates in the fact that they are hard to get used to. Why is this true? Because their secrets get in the way. Of course, healthy people have secrets too, but normally we deal with each other without making these secrets an issue. In the case of the mentally ill, their secrets project out, making them difficult people to deal with.

These ideas represent my thinking before the publication in Japanese of *The Anatomy of Dependence*. Subsequently, my thinking on the concept of the secret progressed rapidly. In 1972, I developed the following argument in an article titled *Seishin byōri to himitsu* (Psychopathology and Secrets).[5] In cases of schizophrenia, the patient feels that there is a trick somewhere by which his or her secret is revealed to the outside and that, because of this, his or her own unique existence has disappeared. On this point, it is similar to the condition of modern man, who has become completely absorbed in external secrets and is unconcerned with the secrets of the inner life.

I later developed my theory of schizophrenia further in a study entitled *Bunretsubyō to himitsu* (Schizophrenia and Secrets),[6] and it was around this time that a new conceptualization of secrets, and an awareness of the extraordinary possibilities of the concept of *omote* and *ura*, began to come together in my mind.

Soon afterwards, I took up the problem of *omote* and *ura* in several speculative essays,[7] in which I suggested that *omote* and *ura* are parallel to the paired concepts of *tatemae* and *honne*, and that they represent a psychology corresponding to the distinction between *soto* and *uchi* in Japanese human relations, which I first introduced in *The Anatomy of Dependence*. I also touched on the possibility of describing psychopathology by using the concepts of *omote* and *ura*.

For example, schizophrenics develop delusions—which themselves can be interpreted as the forms taken by a schizophrenic's secrets that he or she is unable to hold inside—precisely because they are unable to distinguish between *omote* and *ura*, or to make proper use of *tatemae* and *honne*.

In 1973, I published a paper in English on this subject in the *Journal of Nervous and Mental Disease* (see Appendix Two). Finally, in 1976, I published a paper that attempted to deal systematically with the whole question of psychopathology from the perspective of *omote* and *ura*.[8]

At this point, I felt that I had said everything there was to say on the subject from the professional psychiatrist's point of view, at least for the time being, and I began to think about writing a book for the general reader, as I had done with *The Anatomy of Dependence*. But as was true of this earlier work, I had no intention of turning what I had written for specialists into something "easy to understand" for the lay reader. Rather, I wanted to go deeper into something that could perhaps be called the kernel of my own thinking, to flesh things out in ways that go beyond the professional concerns of the clinical psychiatrist.

But I also had no intention of launching right into such a project and, in fact, I took a very casual view, as if I could write a book like this anytime. Thus, it was not until the spring of 1982, I think, that I finally began thinking seriously about the book. But I realized, once I started to write, that the task I had set for myself was difficult indeed. I had no idea how to structure the book. At first, I thought I could simply model it on *The Anatomy of Dependence*, but it became clear immediately that this would not work. In the end, I had to rewrite the manuscript many times before, finally, it took its present form.

The Anatomy of Self is the third book I have written for the general reader. The first, *The Psychological World of Natsume Sōseki (Natsume Sōseki no Shinteki Sekai)*,[9] was first published serially over a period of one year, but it seems to me now that I wrote it in a single moment of intense inspiration. *The Anatomy of Dependence* was based on my own research. While it took some time to come up with a satisfactory format, I don't remember having worked so hard to complete it. *The Anatomy of Self* has been the most difficult of the three. At first I thought I had gotten old. "Had my mind finally begun to slow down?" I thought anxiously. But that doesn't seem to have been the cause of my difficulty. Perhaps that had something to do with it, but the real problem, in my opinion, was the material itself, and the nature of the ideas that I wanted to tackle.

In my book on Sōseki, I could base my work on the ideas and the literary works of one of Japan's most outstanding writers. Of the three, it was the easiest to write. In *The Anatomy of Dependence*, I had to present my own ideas, but I was in previously unexplored territory, and I felt little resistance to writing about what I had discovered there. Writing *The Anatomy of Self* was a completely different experience. The ground had been covered by many other scholars and thinkers before me, and yet I had to decide for myself the course that I would take.

Whether I have in fact succeeded is of course a matter for the reader to decide. As for myself, I am not satisfied; certainly not when I think about the amount of work I put into writing the book. I sometimes have the feeling that I have done nothing more than to restate old ideas and conventional wisdoms in a variety of new arrangements. But I quote here as my own apologia the following words from Pascal:

> Let no one say that I have said nothing new; the arrangement of the material is new. In playing tennis both players use the same ball, but one plays it better.
>
> I would just as soon be told that I have used old words. As if the same thoughts did not form a different argument by being differently arranged, just as the same words make different thoughts when arranged differently![10]

Notes

. Doi Takeo, *The Anatomy of Dependence* (Tokyo: Kodansha International, 1973). Japanese edition, *Amae no Kōzō* (Tokyo: Kōbundō, 1971).

. Doi Takeo, *Seishin Bunseki* [Psychoanalysis] in *Gendai Shinrigaku Taikei* [Compendium of Contemporary Psychology] (Tokyo: Kyōritsu Shuppan, 956), 10:78. See also Doi Takeo, *Seishin Bunseki to Seishin Byōri* [Psychoanalysis and Psychopathology] (Tokyo: Igaku Shoin, 1970), 99.

. Doi Takeo, *Seishin Ryōhō to Seishin Bunseki* [Psychotherapy and

Psychoanalysis] (Tokyo: Kaneko Shobō, 1984).

4. See Doi Takeo, *Naze seishinka ni tsuite henken o motsu ka* [Why Do People Have a Prejudice Against Psychiatry?] in *Seishin Bunseki* [Psychoanalysis] (Tokyo: Sōgen Igaku Shinsho, 1982).

5. Doi Takeo, *Seishin byōri to himitsu* [Psychopathology and Secrets], in *Shisō*, January 1972, 137–140. (This was a review of Professor Murakami Jin's *Seishin Byōrigaku Ronshū* [Collected Papers on Psychopathology].)

6. Doi Takeo, *Bunretsubyō to himitsu* [Schizophrenia and Secrets], in Doi Takeo, ed., *Bunretsubyō no Seishin Byōri* [The Psychopathology of Schizophrenia] (Tokyo: Tokyo University Press, 1972).

7. See Doi Takeo, *Amae Zakkō* [Collected Essays on *Amae*] (Tokyo: Kōbundō, 1975).

8. Doi Takeo, *Omote to ura no seishin byōri* [The Psychopathology of *Omote* and *Ura*] in Ogino Kōichi, ed., *Bunretsubyō no Seishin Byōri* [The Psychopathology of Schizophrenia], vol. 4 (Tokyo: Tokyo University Press, 1976).

9. Doi Takeo, *The Psychological World of Natsume Sōseki*, William Jefferson Tyler, trans. (Cambridge: Harvard University Press, 1976). Japanese edition, *Sōseki no Shinteki Sekai* (Tokyo: Kadokawa Shoten, 1982).

10. Blaise Pascal, *Pensées*, 696, A. J. Krailsheimer, trans., ed. (Middlesex: Penguin Books, 1984), 247. (No. 22 in the Brunschvicq ed.)

PART ONE

BASIC CONCEPTS

Chapter One

Omote and *Ura*

Like their Latin counterparts *recto* and *verso*, *omote* and *ura*[1] are paired opposing concepts. We speak of the *omote-ura* of things, referring to the two sides of everything, and we also use them as opposing concepts in various combinations with other words. An *omote-dōri* is a busy main street; an *ura-dōri* is a lonely back alley. *Omote-muki* refers to that which is public, open, official; *ura-muki* suggests something private, closed, personal. *Omote-ji* is the material used for a kimono or a business suit; *ura-ji* is the material used for the lining. A performer's principal art is his *omote-gei*; *ura-gei* is a hidden talent.

Even when we use them separately, one term implies the other: To speak of *omote* is to speak of *ura*; to speak of *ura* is to speak of *omote*. *Omote o tateru* is "to put up a front." *Omote o tsukurou* is "to keep up appearances." *Omote o haru* means "to keep up a facade." To the Japanese, the allusion to *ura* is implicit in these expressions. Similarly, *ura o miru* means "to see what is behind," or "to see beneath the surface." "To attack from the rear" is *ura o kaku*. In these examples, the allusion to *omote* is also understood. And this dialectical relationship is even more explicit in the saying that "in every *ura* is an *ura*."

I do not know whether there are similar usages in other

languages, but it seems to me that this consciousness of grasping things simultaneously in terms of both their aspects of *omote* and *ura* is especially well-developed in the Japanese language. I say this because I think *omote* and *ura* correspond to the distinction between *soto* (outside) and *uchi* (inside) that is often prominent in the Japanese consciousness of human relations.[2] *Omote* is that which is presented to the *soto*. *Ura* is that which is not presented to *soto*, but kept closed up in *uchi*. Seen in this light, oppositions such as *omote-muki* and *ura-muki*, as well as *omote o tateru* and *ura o miru*, become even clearer. I would not go so far as to say that every phrase in which *ura* or *omote* appears can be explained in terms of this correspondence, but I think the great majority can.

It is also important to note that in classical Japanese *omote* means *kao* (face),[3] and that *ura* means *kokoro* (mind, heart, soul).[4] Since we still use the expression *omote o ageru* ("to raise the face") in formal situations, most Japanese are aware of this connection, but it may not be very widely known that *ura* can mean "mind." In fact, the only use of *ura* by itself to mean mind occurs in the phrase *ura nashi* ("without mind"), an adjective meaning "nonchalant," or "without true intent." Elsewhere, it always appears embedded in combinations with other words. For example, *urayamu* ("to be sick of mind") means "to envy," "to be jealous," or "to yearn for." *Uragiru* ("to cut the mind") means "to betray." *Uramu* ("to see another's hidden mind") means "to bear a grudge," or "to think ill of another person." The meaning of *ura* as mind is also present when it is attached as a prefix to adjectives of emotion. *Uraganashi* and *urasabishi* make it explicit that it is the speaking subject's mind that is sad or lonely.

Since *omote* and *ura* mean "face" and "mind," we can conclude that the relationship between *omote* and *ura* is modeled on the relationship between face and mind and that it is constituted by a generalization and abstraction of that relationship. In the relationship between face and mind, the face usually expresses the mind. When we say that a person's face is "aglow" (*kao ga kagayaite iru*), or that it is "cloudy" (*kao ga kumotte iru*), or that it is "a face deep in thought" (*kangaebukai kao*), we are speaking directly of the face. What we mean, however, although it is expressed indirectly, is the mind as it appears on the face. Of course, the face that we are talking about here is not merely the face as a part of the human body, not simply the face that is seen. It is the face as an object representing a human subject that looks and listens and speaks.

But the face does not necessarily express the mind candidly. As is explicit in the expression "Devil-mask, Buddha-mind" (*kimen busshin*), sometimes the face seems to hide the mind. The face conceals the mind even while expressing it, expresses the mind even while concealing it—so as not to reveal it completely. Perhaps it would be more accurate to say that this simultaneous expression/concealment of the mind by the face is itself the work of the mind. Thus, the relationship between the face and the mind is not a constant, and it is an unmistakable fact that they are in a dyadic relationship.

Seen in this light, it is highly interesting that the English word "person" derives from the Latin word *persona*, which means "an actor's mask." Why do actors wear masks in the first place? Because the mask makes the actor's role clear at a single glance. The mask expresses the actor's role even more directly than an elaborate costume or skillfully contrived makeup. It is for this reason that the list of characters in a play (not the actors) is still called the *dramatis personae*. In this way, *persona*, the actor's mask, came to mean "a role in a play," and then, in English, became "person," a human being.

Although no comparable development can be seen in the Japanese word *o-men* (mask), it is worth noting that in the Nō theater the theatrical mask achieved a unique artistic development that succeeded in pushing the expression of human faces and of human emotion to the outer limits of abstraction.

As we have seen, facial expressions are a complex process, concealing the mind even as they express it, expressing the mind even as they conceal it. The Nō mask stylizes this process. One aspect of facial expression is exaggerated, and everything else is chiseled away. When we say that a person's face is "like a Nō mask" (*nōmen no yō*), we mean that it is expressionless. However, when the mask is actually used in a Nō performance, one responds to the way in which the actor subtly uses the mask to convey different emotions. It is this skillful handling of the mask that produces the effect of *yūgen*,[5] and the ability of the Nō mask to evoke this response can only be described as uncanny.

What I have said about the relationship between the face and the mind can be applied directly to the relationship between *omote* and *ura*. *Omote* can be seen, but *ura* is concealed behind *omote*. However, *omote* does not merely reveal only itself, and neither is it simply something that conceals *ura*. *Omote* is what expresses *ura*. Perhaps we could even say that *ura* performs *omote*. And, because this is true, when people look at *omote*, they are seeing not only *omote*, but also *ura* through *omote*. In fact, it may well be closer to the truth to say that they are looking at *omote* solely in order to see *ura*.

In this way, although *omote* and *ura* are clearly distinguished conceptually, they are in fact closely related. Without *omote* there is no *ura*, without *ura* no *omote*—they are literally two sides (aspects) of a single entity. *Omote* and *ura* do not exist separately but, cojoined, form a single existence. The distinction between them arises from a recognition of this single existence. *Omote* and *ura* are not split; they suggest unity.

Are there other things that correspond to *omote* and *ura*? What about the Western philosophical concept of phenomenon and essence? Phenomenon is the aspect of existence that is present to sight (*eidos*); essence is the special quality (substance, existence, *ousia*) that is in the background of phenomenon and defines it. Phenomenon would thus correspond to *omote*, and essence to *ura*.

In the same way, the relationship between writing (scription) and meaning, or between text and interpretation, can be seen as one of *omote* and *ura*. We may speak of an *omote* meaning and an *ura* meaning in textual interpretation itself. The Edo-period *waka* poet Fujitani Mitsue (1768–1823) employed exactly these terms in interpreting poetry. In his *Kojiki Tomoshibi* (Lamp on the *Kojiki*), published in 1808, Fujitani criticized Motoori Norinaga for looking only at the *omote* of words and for failing to realize that the most Japanese of all things lay in that which was concealed.[6] Norinaga (1730–1801) had already used *omote* and *ura* in *Shibun Yōryō* (The Essence of the Murasaki Text), his famous treatise on *The Tale of Genji*. This treatise was completed in 1763, so we may well imagine that the use of *omote* and *ura* in a double sense is quite old. The following is from the introduction to Norinaga's analysis of the "*Hotaru*" (Fireflies) chapter of the tale:

> Now, in this episode, which begins with "[they each told tales] of outlandish things that had happened to people,"—from where Genji says, "Ah, how depressing. Women [are born with a genius for being deceived by people and never finding it a bore.]"—Murasaki Shikibu is ostensibly telling the story of a chat between Prince Genji and Lady Tamakazura. In fact, she is stating her intention [*kokorobae*] in writing *The Tale of Genji*. Therefore, in this episode, although the surface [*omote*] is merely part of the tale of Prince Genji and Lady Tamakazura, the underlying intention [*shita no kokoro*] is Murasaki Shikibu's basic interpretation of the entire tale she has written. Even where the *omote* is fabricated as verbal play, the un-

derlying intention [*kokoro*] has meaning throughout. It is this intention that praises or disparages the tale, exalts and debases it, and then states a conclusion. Moreover, the prose style in this episode is not intense, but an easy style that flows quite smoothly. Murasaki Shikibu did not write this passage at the beginning of the tale, or at the end, but instead, in a rather insignificant part of the text, gradually making the reader aware of her overall intention. And though she does not gratuitously state that this is her intention, she has written in such a way as to make the reader hear it for what it is. This deserves to be called the work of genius, unparalled either in our country or in China.

As I have said, there have been many commentaries, but these are merely perfunctory notes on the surface [*omote*] meaning of the text. It is difficult for the author's true intention to reveal itself in them. Moreover, many of these commentaries are mistaken in their interpretations. They grossly violate the author's true intention, and fail to grasp the meaning of the text. Therefore, I shall now explain the passage in detail, basing my interpretation on a clear distinction between the *omote* meaning of the text and the *ura* meaning. Those who read this commentary should take great care. Understand the distinction between the *omote* meaning and the *ura* meaning, which includes the underlying intentionality [*shita no kokoro*]. Do not confuse them.[7]

In this last example, *omote* and *ura* indicate a two-fold meaning. I believe that ultimately this is the same thing as employing the concept of *omote* and *ura* to suggest the double-sidedness of things. Interestingly, the dual oppositions of phenomenon/essence and text/interpretation that I have suggested above as examples of concepts corresponding to *omote* and *ura* do not suggest this double-sidedness in the same way. This could be due to the fact that the concept of *omote* and *ura*, simple as it may appear at first glance, also implies the problem of point of view.

Omote is the side that is visible to the eye; *ura* is the side that is not. Therefore, when the point of view shifts, *omote* and *ura* may be transposed. There is nothing strange about this. This becomes even clearer when considered in light of the fact that *omote* and *ura* correspond to *soto* and *uchi* in human relations. That is, since *soto* and *uchi* are different for each individual, what is *soto* for one person may become *uchi* for a person included in that *soto*. Clearly, the former's *omote* becomes the latter's *ura*. In this sense, *omote* and *ura* are extremely relative, and it is for this reason that they suggest a quality of two-sidedness.

As we have seen, the Japanese actually use—and use frequently—ways of speaking that signify the two aspects of *omote* and *ura* in things. And even if these two aspects are contradictory at the level of words, they are both true. This is the result of differing points of view. Moreover, Japanese usually do not make an issue of the fact that there is a lack of logical consistency between the two. Perhaps this is because we give precedence to the logic of *omote* and *ura* over logical consistency in language. In any case, most Japanese are not very attentive to using words analytically, and neither are they very enthusiastic about relying on logical consistency.

Words are totally monothetic, and most of them are used with implied value judgments of good and bad. At present, words such as freedom and equality are good; discrimination and authority are not good. Normally, what is thought to be good is displayed in *omote*. What we fear may be judged negatively is shut away in *ura*. This point applies best to cases of *tatemae* and *honne*, which will be discussed more fully in the next chapter.

A note of caution may be necessary here. I have said that Japanese often speak of the double-sided nature of things, and that they are not much concerned with contradictions at the level of language, but I do not mean to suggest that this is always true. There are any number of Japanese who insist on seeing only one side of things. By the same token, to point out that Westerners excel at using words analytically is not to say that all Westerners do so. Indeed, there seems to be a great deal in common between the Japanese awareness of the double-sidedness of things and the Western consciousness of the dual meanings of words.

Consider, for example, the case of *amae*.[8] When we say that it is not good to exhibit *amae* behavior (*amaeru*) outside (in the *soto*) but that it is all right if one is inside (*uchi*), we are using the logic of *omote* and *ura*. However, in this statement, even though we use the same word in describing both cases of *amae* behavior, the meaning of *amae* can be said to be fundamentally different. That is, we can say that gratuitous, self-centered *amae* is a completely different thing from the *amae* that develops naturally in an intimate relationship. When we do so, we are also pointing out the duality of the word *amae*.

We do the same thing with the word nature. When we speak of the providence of Nature, or say that the Japanese revere Nature in all things, we signify a natural order that we believe to be the fountainhead of all existence. However, words such as natural instincts, natural drives, and Nature's child, signify conditions that are opposed to norms. It is possible to think of this double meaning in the word nature not merely as a problem of language, but also as an indication of the duality of that existence we call nature itself.

We have discussed the double-sidedness of things, and the problem of language. Here, I would like to consider this problem of words and meaning once again, this time from the perspective of *omote* and *ura*. For it is possible to say that words are *omote*, that they conceal/express and express/conceal the mind (*kokoro*), which is *ura*. That words express the mind requires no explanation, but how do words conceal the mind? The phrase "to save appearances" (*omote o tsukurou*) provides a good example. It means to put up a good front so that what is concealed will not be found out.

Words both express and conceal the mind, and so does the face, but these two acts of expression/concealment are not always concurrent. In not a few cases we may deny something with words, but a glance, or the set of the lips, betray our words, expressing precisely what they have denied. We could even say that one's facial expressions are more honest than words. On the other hand, words provide a much larger quantity of information, though it must also be said that the more there is expressed the more there is that is concealed.

In this way, words conceal the mind even as they express it, but this act of concealment is by no means limited to deliberate concealment. Every time we say something, we also conceal, in the instant we put it into words, everything outside it, by choosing not to put it into words. This is an extremely selective act. There are also times when we find ourselves trying to say something that is difficult to express in words. Japanese have an expression for the feeling that arises in this situation: "Somehow, when I try to put it into words, it sounds like a lie." The act of using words is always accompanied by a partial shadowing. Depending on the way we look at it, we could almost say that it is actually from out of the shadows that words emerge.

We can also replace the word shadows with silence. The great Swiss philosopher Max Picard's work on silence is extremely interesting. I would like to share a few passages from his *The World of Silence* here:

Language and silence belong together: language has knowledge of silence as silence has knowledge of language.

* * *

Whenever a man begins to speak, the word comes from silence at each new beginning.

It comes so self-evidently and so unobtrusively as if it were merely the reverse of silence, merely silence turned around. Speech is in fact the reverse of silence, just as silence is the reverse of speech.

* * *

Silence can exist without speech, but speech cannot exist without silence. The word would be without depth if the background of silence were missing.

* * *

Silence is fulfilled only when speech comes forth from silence.

* * *

Silence is present in language, therefore, even after language has arisen out of silence.[9]

These brief passages alone are enough to make it clear that what Picard describes as the relationship between words and silence is the same relationship that I have analyzed in terms of *omote* and *ura*.

One of the few Westerners to have argued for the significance of silence, Picard was, however, by no means guilty of underrating words, as the brief passages below indicate:

Truth is the scaffolding that gives language an independent foothold over against silence.

* * *

Truth is present as an objective reality in the logic of language. . . .[10]

As these passages suggest, the Western philosophical tradition is suffused with an emphasis on the importance of words. In Japan, such a tradition does not exist. I do not mean to suggest that traditional Japanese thought makes light of words, but it seems to be more conscious of matters that words do not reach. Interestingly, this consciousness is often grounded in a keen sensitivity to words. The fact that the Japanese have always privileged reserve over eloquence is based on the same mentality. To be sure, it would be a mistake to think that this tendency is to be seen only among the Japanese. The same sensibility exists in any number of other people.

With Picard in mind, I would like to return to the problem of the double-sidedness of things. When *omote* and *ura* are reversed—when what was at first not expressed in words *is* expressed—it is natural that the words of that expression should contradict the words that were spoken first. It is for this reason that Japanese are not overly concerned when the two aspects of something contradict each other at the level of language. Of course, this must not lead to the conclusion that the Japanese are nonchalant about deception. To the Japanese, a person who presents an artificial front in order to deceive others is a "person with *ura-omote*." Such a description is always critical. But to be Japanese is to be aware of the fact that things have an *omote* and an *ura*, and a person is not considered to be an adult until he or she has grasped this distinction.

Notes

1. *Omote* 表. *Ura* 裏.

2. *Soto* 外 and *uchi* 内 constitute a dyadic pair that is close to "outside-inside" in English. This is clear in the contrast made in human relations between *soto no hito* (outsiders) 外の人 and *uchi no hito* (insiders) 内の人. Again, however, the sociological implications of this structure differ from those suggested by the English concepts, and I prefer to retain the Japanese terms.

3. *Kao* 顔.

4. *Kokoro* 心. The English terms given are all very close to *kokoro*, and the ambiguous relationships among them are also encompassed by the Japanese term. *Shinrigaku* 心理学, the Japanese term for psychology, is literally "the study of the principles of *kokoro*." But *shinzō* 心臓, the anatomical term for the heart, is "the storehouse of *kokoro*." The significance of this concept in Japanese is manifest in the fact that the Chinese character for *kokoro* is also the radical of almost all characters with meanings related to thought or emotion. For example, *i* 意 is the character for "intention," and *nasake* 情 is the character for "human feeling."

5. [*Yūgen* 幽玄 is one of the key concepts of Japanese aesthetics. Originally borrowed from China, it underwent a unique development in Japan, its meaning gradually changing through the centuries. Zeami (1364?–1443), the great playwright and theorist of the Nō, saw the beauty of *yūgen* in the famous ladies of the Heian court, or in their fictional counterparts, which has led Konishi Jinichi to define *yūgen* as "mysterious elegance and beauty." For an exposition of the development of *yūgen*, see Professor Konishi's *A History of Japanese Literature* (Princeton: Princeton University Press, 1985), 1:14.—Trans.]

6. [Both men were instrumental in the formation of *kokugaku* (national studies), the great pre-modern tradition of philology. See Umitani Fumio, *Jugaku to Kokugaku* [Confucian Studies and National Studies], in Ichiko Teiji and Tsutsumi Seiji, eds., *Nihon Bungaku Zenshi* [Complete History of Japanese Literature], 4 (Tokyo: Gakutōsha, 1979), 258–276.—Trans.]

7. Motoori Norinaga, *Shibun Yōryō*, in *Motoori Norinaga Shū, Shinchō Nihon Koten Shūsei* (Shinchō Compendium of the Japanese Classics), Vol. 60 (Tokyo: Shinchō-sha, 1983), 75–76. [Editor's Note: All translations from the Japanese are those of the translator. Wherever possible, bibliographic information has been provided for readers interested in a complete translation.]

8. Readers who have read *The Anatomy of Dependence* will be familiar with the concept of *amae*. Briefly stated, *amae* refers to passive dependence, or passive love, and manifests itself in the desire to be indulged by the object of *amae*. Like many Japanese words, *amae*, a noun, can become *amaeru*, a verb meaning "to exhibit *amae* behavior."

9. Max Picard, *The World of Silence*, Stanley Godman, trans. (South Bend, Indiana: Regnery/Gateway, Inc., 1952), 16, 24, 28, 29, 37.

10. Ibid., 32, 33.

Chapter Two

Tatemae and *Honne*

Japanese have begun using the dyadic concepts of *tatemae* and *honne* quite frequently, often with the implication that *tatemae* is directed solely at *omote* and therefore false, and that only *honne* is the real truth. Indeed, so strong is this implication that when we say something is only *tatemae* we are in fact denying its value. Only after *honne* presents itself do we feel that we are on secure ground. But there is reason to believe that this was not always true.

First, consider the etymology of the word *tatemae*. It is beyond doubt that the *tatemae* of *tatemae-honne* was originally the same word as the word *tatemae* in Japanese architecture, which means "raising the ridgepole."[1] This work was considered to be so important that the owner of the building under construction would treat the master builder and his helpers to a lavish banquet after it was completed. *Tatemae* is also the word used in the tea ceremony for the formal movements of the host in presenting utensils and serving the tea.[2] In both architecture and the tea ceremony, the *tatemae* is essential; without it, the building could not be built, the tea ceremony could not be performed. If the *tatemae* of *tatemae-honne* is indeed the same word, it is impossible to believe that it is unimportant.

In fact, dictionary definitions of *tatemae* define it as a type of principles or rules that have been established as natural and proper. Such principles and rules are of course important. For example, the use of *tatemae* in Kabuki refers to the fact that play scripts were composed according to established conventions. But these rules or conventions are established by people and can therefore be overturned by people. This may be related to the sensibility expressed by the phrase "that is only *tatemae*."

We can also approach this problem by looking at modern usages of the word *tatemae*. Here are some examples:

> The system requiring all students to live in dormitories is the *tatemae* at this school.

> We uphold the *tatemae* of equality between the sexes.

> It has been decided that, as the *tatemae*, Japan will not maintain war capabilities.

Quite by chance, I discovered the following statement made by Kinoshita Mokutarō (1885–1945) in a round-table discussion on scientific technology and literature during the war:

> Since it is no doubt impossible for most people to understand by its name alone what kind of *tatemae* this thing called the "science novel" has, I think it is first necessary to clearly define its boundaries.[3]

This statement also suggests that *tatemae* refers to conventions created by people on the basis of consensus. Seen in this light, it is even more clear that the *tatemae* under discussion here originally had the same meaning as *tatemae* in architecture or the tea ceremony. In short, *tatemae* always implies the existence of a group of people in its background who assent to it.

In contrast to this, *honne* refers to the fact that the individuals who belong to the group, even while they consent to the *tatemae*, each have their own motives and opinions that are distinct from it, and that they hold these in its background. In fact, these individual, personal ways of viewing the *tatemae* can themselves be said to be *honne*.

While *tatemae* appears in *omote*, *honne* is concealed in *ura*. Therefore, what has been said above about the relationship between *omote* and *ura* also applies to the relationship between *tatemae* and *honne*. That is, *honne* exists only because there is *tatemae*, and *honne* manipulates *tatemae* from behind. In this way, *tatemae* and *honne* are in a mutually defining and mutually constituting relationship. Without one, the other cannot exist.

Consider once more the analogy of *tatemae* in architecture. We could argue that raising the ridgepole itself is not the real aim, but rather the framework of the *tatemae* is constructed in order to cover it with a roof and walls, and to support the floor of the building. But it could also be argued that it is possible to raise the roof, add walls, and lay the flooring only after the foundation has been laid and the *tatemae* constructed. The relationship between *tatemae* and *honne* works by the same logic.

As a more concrete example, consider the case of a news media campaign to stir up popular opinion. These campaigns are permitted because freedom of speech is guaranteed by the constitution. In this sense, freedom of speech is the *tatemae* of mass communication. But when a given news organization launches a media campaign on a given issue, it may be because the company secretly wants to manipulate popular opinion in ways that will prove profitable to itself; or, because the reporter or editor in charge wants a promotion. In this case, Japanese would refer to these hidden motives by saying that they are the *honne* of the situation.

To avoid any misunderstanding, I should point out here that I do not mean to suggest by the above example that *tatemae* is morally good and *honne* morally evil. Nor do I want to say that *honne* is the truth and *tatemae* mere pretense. Rather, I am attempting to demonstrate that it is inherent in the relationship between *tatemae* and *honne* that they are mutually constitutive. One does not exist without the other. Speaking in terms of the previous example, freedom of speech is predicated upon the expectation that individuals will actually say whatever they like, and guarantees their right to do so within the political *tatemae* of freedom of speech. Therefore, to the extent that we observe this *tatemae* of freedom of speech, anyone may indeed speak on the basis of his or her own *honne*.

This analysis can be related to Weber's concept of legitimate order. In *The Theory of Social and Economic Organization*, Weber writes, "The subjective meaning of a social relationship will be called an 'order' only if action is approximately or on the average ordered to some determinate 'maxims' or rules," and further that, "naturally, in concrete cases, the orientation of action to an order involves a wide range of motives."[4] Clearly, Weber's "legitimate order" corresponds to *tatemae* and his "wide range of motives" to *honne*.

Weber goes on to discuss various types of legitimate order and their bases, but his analysis does not touch on the point that order legitimizes action and that, in doing so, permits the existence of the "wide range of motives" that are concealed in action, although this is certainly implied by his theory. In any case, what is most important in the relationship between *tatemae* and *honne* is the fact that the former legitimizes the latter. It is interesting indeed that the Japanese concepts can be related to Weber's theory through his definition of legitimization.

However, it is essential to note here that the individual is not always self-consciously aware of the distinction between *tatemae* and *honne*. Take the case of a male teacher who is especially earnest in teaching one of his female students. Since it is his job to teach, we may interpret his actions as those of a teacher faithfully observing the *tatemae* of his profession. But a careful investigation of his speech and behavior might reveal that, in fact, he secretly has deeper feelings for the student. If he is clearly aware of these feelings, then they are his *honne*. But it is also conceivable that he will insist that he is only doing his job and has no *honne* at all in this situation.

The same thing may be said of a housewife who is unusually enthusiastic about volunteer work. On the one hand, of course, she is enthusiastic because her consciousness has been raised and she wants to make a contribution to society. But her enthusiasm might also be the result of trouble at home; or perhaps she just wants to get out of the house and away from the everyday tasks of housework and taking care of her family. In some cases she will be clearly conscious of these motives as her own *honne*; in others she will be unable to recognize them.

Similarly, when a person who is normally shy and retiring suddenly begins denouncing others in the name of justice, it is almost certain that he or she is conscious only of the *tatemae* (in this case "justice") and believes that there is no *honne* other than that *tatemae*. Whenever something is done in the name of justice—whether it is launching a world war or merely a media campaign—it is no exaggeration to say that the people involved are almost never aware of their own *honne* as *honne*.

I want to emphasize once again that in citing these concrete cases I do not mean to suggest that *tatemae* is "good" and *honne* "evil." Moreover, since it is the nature of things that *tatemae* is revealed to the outside and that *honne* is not revealed, there is nothing inherently wrong in the fact that *honne* is concealed within (in *uchi*).

It is quite a different matter when a person does not recognize his or her own *honne* for what it is and actually goes so far as to deny its existence. When this happens, the person loses control of *honne* and, as a result, *honne* can run rampant in ways that are extremely grotesque. As I suggested above, *tatemae* legitimizes *honne*. But, in this case, difficulties arise because that legitimization is emphasized so strongly that the person loses sight of the very existence of *honne*.

This condition corresponds to what is called rationalization in psychoanalysis: a condition in which instinctual impulses are justified not as impulses that thrust up from below but as something rational. In more general terms, it is the mentality of those who say that "the end justifies the means." Once this mentality is established, once it is decided that as long as the end is good, the means no longer matter, the means escalate apace. And it is at this point that we arrive at the worst possible scenario, in which evil is committed in the name of good.

As the analysis above suggests, there are aspects of *tatemae* and *honne* that may be understood in terms of concepts imported from the West: Weber's "legitimate order," rationalization in psychoanalytic theory, the ethical concepts of means and ends, the contrastive pair of public and private. Nevertheless, it is undeniable that the pairing of *tatemae* and *honne* is a uniquely Japanese way of thinking and, indeed, of feeling.

In Weber's concept, "legitimate order" and the "wide range of motives" that are at work when individuals orient their actions to it are clearly distinguished and never intersect. The concept of *tatemae-honne* is extremely vague on this point. Of course, when we say *tatemae* and *honne*, we clearly distinguish the two as concepts. But it is essential to note that the two terms are being used to describe a single thing, with an implicit prior understanding that the two aspects of *tatemae* and *honne* constitute a single reality.

The characteristic feature of the relationship between *tatemae* and *honne* is that *tatemae* conceals *honne* even as it represents *honne*. The English words public and private, which correspond to *ōyake* and *watakushi* in Japanese, signify realms that are strictly distinguished. As such, they never overlap. In contrast to this, *tatemae* and *honne* coexist as two contiguous principles. Depending on which one is emphasized, the two aspects of public (*ōyake*) and private (*watakushi*) may rise to the surface in turns. This relationship can only be described as extremely curious.

I believe that the Japanese have actually thought about human affairs in terms of the dyadic concepts of *tatemae* and *honne* throughout much of their history. To be sure, the words themselves are relatively new. In fact, there is evidence suggesting that they came into frequent use only after World War Two. As I pointed out in the previous chapter, however, *omote* and *ura*, which correspond to *tatemae* and *ura*, have been used since ancient times, and if it is indeed true that the Japanese have always had this tendency to grasp things in terms of the two aspects of *omote* and *ura*, the substance of *tatemae* and *honne* must also have existed.

In this connection, it is interesting to note Allessandro Valignano's observations concerning the Japanese near the end of the sixteenth century, in which he listed the following as one of the defects of the Japanese:

> As they do not know the difference between the prudence of the flesh, and the world, and genuine prudence, they fall into this error, attributing to prudence the state of being misleading, and showing themselves in the exterior in such a way that it is impossible to understand what they have in their hearts. If only they would modify this characteristic in accordance with genuine prudence it would be praiseworthy indeed, for in this respect, they deal more thoughtfully than we do in many matters. They know how to keep quiet and dissemble when the occasion calls for it, and from this, many benefits would follow if only, as I have said, this prudence would not exceed the boun-

daries of reason. But because the Japanese cannot restrain this habit, prudence becomes a vice; they become so deceptive that they can be understood only with the greatest difficulty, and it is quite impossible to know by their words and outward signs what they are feeling and thinking in their hearts.[5]

This statement is all the more interesting because Valignano also praised the Japanese for their highly developed sense of ethics. Luis Frois, a contemporary of Valignano, was probably referring to the same phenomenon when he wrote in his *Da Historia de Japam 1549–1582* that the Japanese are fond of ambiguous language and complained of their "false smiles."[6]

The phenomenon of *tatemae* and *honne* was recognized much earlier in Kenkō's *Tsurezuregusa*, which is thought to have been compiled in the first half of the fourteenth century. Kenkō describes a scene in which an easterner criticizes the people of Kyoto for making excellent promises they have no intention of fulfilling:

> Gyōren Shōnin, abbot of the temple of Hidenin, whose secular name was Miura something or other, was an unrivaled warrior. A person from his native place came to visit him and, in the course of his stories about home, said, "It is people from the East whose words can be trusted. As for the people of the capital, only their promises are good, but there is no truth to them." The holy man clarified the principles of the matter thus: "You no doubt believe this to be true, but I have lived in the capital for a long time and have become well acquainted with the people, and I do not believe their hearts to be inferior. It is because in general their hearts are gentle and they have human sympathy that they find it difficult to say no to what

another has said, that they cannot speak out about everything they are thinking, and that they meekly make promises. They do not mean to deceive, but since they are poor and in straitened circumstances, there are doubtless many things in which they cannot carry through their own true intentions [*honne*]. The people of the East are my own compatriots, but, in truth, their hearts are not kind, and because they are a blunt and unaffable people, they do not hesitate to say no from the very beginning. It is because of their prosperity and wealth that they are trusted by others."[7]

In modern terms, the abbot's defense amounts to this: Kyoto people speak in this way only because they are expressing *tatemae*. It is mistaken to believe that this is hypocrisy. Instead, one should see in their attempts to construct a *tatemae* evidence of their real sincerity.

To a certain extent, these observations concerning the people of Kyoto would apply to a comparison of the Japanese people as a whole, who deal with everything in terms of *tatemae* and *honne*, to foreigners. Certainly, this way of dealing with others reduces interpersonal friction between people to a minimum. And it is perhaps for this reason that the Japanese are particularly fond of subtle considerations and delicate nuances in human relations.

The Japanese discovery of *tatemae* and *honne* may be explained by relating it to the mentality of *amae*. Just as a child displays *amae* toward its parents, *amae* behavior is natural, and the pattern of relationship in which no one would find *amae* strange is that of *uchi*. Counterpoised against these relationships are those of *soto*, in which one is permitted to bring *amae* emotions into relationships on the basis of certain understandings, or conventions. These understandings constitute the *tatemae* of the relationship; that is, since *tatemae* links people together on the basis of a mutual agreement (which is called *tatemae*), *amae* is allowed to operate within the limits of that agreement. In other words, it is possible to see a given *tatemae* as a sign that *amae* is working in the group in which that *tatemae* is honored. The intentions or motives that substantiate these feelings of *amae* are the *honne* of that relationship.

The essential linkage that exists between *tatemae* and *honne* should be quite clear, and I would now like to turn to a more detailed discussion of how these two concepts function as a dyadic pair. This can best be accomplished, I think, by beginning with the meaning of the sign, to which I referred in saying that *tatemae* is a sign that *amae* is working. A sign has two sides, one positive and the other negative. When we say that something is "nothing more than a sign," we are refusing to recognize the intrinsic value of the thing itself. Indeed, in this case, the word sign becomes a virtual pronoun for something worthless. But when we say "a sign of friendship," or "a sign of love," the sign itself is given great significance. Why the value given the sign may increase or decline in this way will become clear if we imagine the following situation.

When presenting a gift to someone, Japanese often say, "This is merely a small token." The giver of the gift means that he wants the other person to accept the gift not for its value but as something expressing his or her feelings (*kokoro*). In such a situation, however, if the recipient of the gift does not believe that the gift-giver's intentions are sincere, the gift really is nothing more than a sign, and in some cases it may appear to be an outright sham. Thus, the sign may gain or lose significance depending on whether the spiritual reality it implies is believed or not.

Ultimately, the fact that *tatemae* is sometimes taken seriously and sometimes not works by the same logic. When we believe in the consensus that is expressed by *tatemae*, we are content to entrust our *honne* to that *tatemae*. But if we do not believe in the *tatemae*, we play it down, putting more weight on our own *honne*. When this happens we must make use of both with careful discrimination.

The dual structure constituted by *tatemae* and *honne* fulfills a major role in maintaining psychic balance. We could even describe it as the sense of balance itself. Again, this point can best be explained by beginning with the psychology of *amae*. By its very nature, *amae* depends on the *other*, on the object of *amae*, and in this sense it is inherently unstable.

When the desire for *amae* is frustrated—that is, when a person wishes to *amaeru* but is not allowed to do so by the other—*amae* can easily switch to resentment. Perhaps we can even say that *amae* conceals the possibility of resentment from the very beginning, and, conversely, that when resentment appears overtly it is concealing *amae*. In psychoanalytic theory, this is called a love-hate condition, and it corresponds to the concept of ambivalence.

A person who has only *amae*, with no other support, is in danger of falling into a condition of ambivalence. As long as one observes *tatemae*, one can depend on the good will of others, and the desire for *amae* is fulfilled, at least to that extent. In this sense, *tatemae* manifests itself as an effective support for *amae*. Motives or intentions that cannot be dealt with by *tatemae* are then shut away inside as *honne*. Ambivalence is thereby structuralized, and, in that form, tolerated. That is, once we become consciously aware of the dual structure of *tatemae* and *honne*, ambivalence is not left to the unconscious where it becomes impossible to control. This is why we are able to say that the dual structure of *tatemae* and *honne* protects psychic balance.

In fact, if *tatemae* and *honne* do not function together in this way, human relations are apt to become awkward. Above, we looked at situations in which people were not able to recognize their own *honne* even when it was present. In other cases, complications arise when *tatemae* and *honne* do not function well together, a situation that I will have more to say about in the following chapter.

I would like to conclude this chapter by saying a word about how the dual structure of *tatemae* and *honne* is formed. Essentially, it develops in the home environment during infancy and childhood and, later, through the human relations developed in school and social situations outside the home. Seen in this light, *tatemae* and *honne* overlap with the psychological and sociological concepts of socialization and self-consciousness. *Tatemae* is precisely a product of socialization, and *honne* is the expression of self-consciousness. Moreover, as G. H. Mead argues in his seminal study of the individual and society, socialization and self-consciousness are intimately related; indeed, they are two sides of the same coin. The following are perhaps his most famous statements on the formation of the self:

> To be self-conscious is essentially to become an object to one's self in virtue of one's social relations to other individuals.
>
> *   *   *
>
> The "I" reacts to the self which arises through the taking of the attitudes of others. Through taking these attitudes we have introduced the "we" and we react to it as an "I."[8]

Mead's concept of "self" corresponds to *tatemae*, and his "to become an object to one's self" is related to the formation of *tatemae*. His "I" is similarly related to *honne*. This may seem to suggest that the Japanese words can be translated into Western concepts. But *tatemae* and *honne* spring from everyday language, and, furthermore, in the inner recesses of their minds, the Japanese are always aware of the special relationship between them. It is this that makes *tatemae* and *honne* so uniquely characteristic of the Japanese and Japanese society.

Notes

1. This use of the word *tatemae* 建前 can refer either to the physical act of raising the ridgepole, which marks the completion of the framework of the house, or to the celebrations that follow. Some traditionally minded Japanese still observe this custom.

2. The Chinese characters for *tatemae* 点前 in the tea ceremony are different from those used for *tatemae* 建前 in architecture or in the *tatemae-honne* 建前-本音 concept itself, but the terms are obviously related.

3. Kinoshita Mokutarō, *Kagaku Gijutsu to Bungaku—Zadankai* [Round Table Discussion on Scientific Technology and Literature], *Kinoshita Mokutarō Zenshū* [The Collected Works of Kinoshita Mokutarō] (Tokyo: Iwanami Shoten, 1983), 25:478.

4. Max Weber, *The Theory of Social and Economic Organization*, A. M. Henderson and Talcott Parsons, trans. (New York: The Free Press, 1964), 124.

5. Alessandro Valignano, *Historia del Principio y Progresso de la Campaña de Jesu's en las Indias Orientales, 1542–1564*, 140. [Translation by Michael Cooper (personal correspondence)—Trans.] See also, Michael Cooper, ed., *They Came to Japan* (Berkeley: University of California Press, 1965), 46, 48n. [Valignano also lists the following as defects: addiction to sensual vices and sins, meager loyalty toward their rulers, and cruelty.—Trans.]

6. Luis Frois, *Segunda Parte da Historia de Japam 1578–1582*, J. A. Abranches Pinto and Y. Okamoto, eds. (Tokyo, 1938) [cited in Cooper, *They Came to Japan*.—Trans.] See also, Matsuda Kiichi and Englebert Jorissen, *Furoisu no Nihon Oboegaki* [The Japan Memoranda of Luis Frois] (Tokyo: Chūō Kōron, 1983).

7. Yoshida Kenkō, *Tsurezuregusa*, episode 141, in *Shinchō Nihon Koten Shūsei* (Shinchō Compendium of the Japanese Classics), vol. 10 (Tokyo: Shinchō-sha, 1977), 162–163. [For a complete English translation, see Donald Keene, trans., *Essays in Idleness* (New York: Columbia University Press, 1967), 127–128.—Trans.]

8. G. H. Mead, *Mind, Self and Society* (Chicago: The University of Chicago Press, 1934), 172, 174.

Chapter Three

Institutions and the Individual

So far, we have discussed the dyadic oppositions, or "contrastive sets," of *omote-ura* and *tatemae-honne*, and I have suggested that the dualistic structures represented by these oppositions are above all profoundly related to the psychology of *amae*. We may also say that it is precisely for this reason that, in Japanese society, people invariably speak in terms of the *omote* and *ura* of things, and that they deal with human affairs in general in terms of the dual structure of *tatemae* and *honne*. Of course, I cannot state positively that this phenomenon can be observed only in Japan, but I think it can at least be said that people are clearly conscious of it in Japanese society.

It is well known, for example, that there are, in both government offices and private firms, personal cliques (*jinmyaku*) that are distinct from human relations based on the organization's job-classification system. In the realm of politics, there have existed throughout Japanese history mechanisms by which the de facto holders of power participate in government concurrently with the court officials directly connected to emperors. Even today, though the *omote* system is democracy based on majority rule, it is common knowledge that a "black curtain" (*kuromaku*) conceals the *ura* of politics, and that a great number of decisions are actually made in behind-the-scenes deals (*kakehiki*) involving manipulation of "old boy" networks and personal connections (*nemawashi*).[1] In fact, some political scientists have apparently begun to describe Japanese politics as a "*tatemae* and *omote* system," or as an "*amae* system."[2]

But there is an interesting parallel between the Japanese concepts of *omote-ura* and *tatemae-honne* and the Western concepts of institutions and the individual. Up to now, we have been considering the Japanese concepts by comparing them to the Western ones. But the concepts of institutions and the individual themselves can be considered in terms of *tatemae-honne* and *omote-ura*, and perhaps we can reinterpret them from the perspective of the Japanese concepts.

First, it is worth noting that the words themselves have similar etymologies. The English word institution comes from Latin, where it was derived from a verb (*instituere*) meaning "to stand [something] up" (*tateru*), "to set," or "to place." Clearly, the first of these is close to the original meaning of *tatemae*. In actual usage, however, *tatemae* sometimes gives a rather light feeling, as in "that's only the *tatemae*," whereas institution always has a weighty feeling.

The same comparison can be made between Japanese and Western architecture. In Japan, buildings are traditionally constructed of wood and quickly deteriorate or burn down. In the West, they are built of stone and are made to endure for hundreds of years. In any case, when we speak of *tatemae*, perhaps because it is established by group consensus, the word somehow suggests something temporary or contingent. In contrast, the word institution refers to permanent *social* institutions. The American sociologist Charles Horton Cooley, for example, describes the concept of institutions in the following manner:

> Language, government, the church, laws and customs of property and of the family, systems of industry and

education, are institutions because they are the working out of permanent needs of human nature.[3]

A careful reading of this description will reveal, however, that the word institution also implies that some form of consensus has been "worked out," and on this point it is no different from *tatemae*. That is, even if they may appear at first glance to be something permanent, institutions are established on the basis of consensus among individuals, and are therefore subject to change. And institutions have in fact undergone constant change throughout the long ages up to the present.

If institutions are essentially the same thing as *tatemae*—the *omote* of society, as it were—it is possible to offer the following hypothesis. That is, just as the face signifies the mind of an individual, institutions, as the face of a society, reveal the characteristic features of that society. If here we consider the concept of culture, and define social institutions as that part of a culture that is enduring and does not change very much, it is possible to say that institutions reflect the unique aspects of the various cultures in which they appear. I would like to consider this hypothesis below in terms of politics and language, examining how these two institutions reveal culturally distinctive features.

In discussing political institutions, I want to compare Japan and the United States. Consider first the famous opening passage of the American *Declaration of Independence*:

> We hold these truths to be self-evident, that all men are created equal, that they are endowed by their Creator with certain unalienable rights, that among these are Life, Liberty, and the pursuit of Happiness. That to secure these rights, Governments are instituted among Men, deriving their just powers from the consent of the governed.[4]

Needless to say, this passage extols the fundamental principles of democracy. But it also expresses the uniquely American philosophy of individualism and optimism that provides the foundation for these principles.

Perhaps the most vital point in the *Declaration of Independence* is the assertion that "all men are created equal." I say this because it is in fact highly doubtful that all people are created equal, and even if they are, it still remains to be asked just how they are equal. Rather, it is fair to suggest that Americans promote equality precisely because of what is in fact an extremely naive belief in universal equality as a self-evident truth. It is in this belief that a uniquely American optimism manifests itself, and it is this belief that provides the groundwork for American-style individualism. If everyone is equal, then each individual must make his or her own way, relying on nothing but his or her own ability. No one else, not even parents, can be depended on.

Alexis de Tocqueville observed the reverse side of this American love for individual autonomy in the early days of the new republic, describing a tendency that can easily become pervasive when public opinion is formed by a majority in which everyone has been made equal. That is, individualism and conformism become two sides of the same coin.[5] This probably occurs because self-determination in all things is in fact impossible, and without a tradition or some authority to rely on, the individual ultimately has no choice but to go along with everyone else.

In this way, it is possible to discover the unique character of American culture in the document that established the basic theory of American politics. We can do the same thing in the case of Japan. The first clause of Article One of the postwar constitution concerns the status of the emperor:

The Emperor shall be the symbol of the state and of

the unity of the people, deriving his position from the will of the people with whom resides sovereign power.[6]

I know virtually nothing about the debates that are taking place among specialists in constitutional law concerning this clause, but in view of the fact that this is the very first clause of the new constitution, I firmly believe that, far from denying Japan's ancient traditions and institutions, this constitution actually upholds a position that respects them before all else—not only for Japan's own people but also for the rest of the world to see. Considering the fact that it was established immediately after defeat in World War Two and, moreover, that it was forced on Japan by the Occupation, it is almost incredible that such a stance could be taken.

Of course, the postwar constitution did not make the emperor an object of religious respect, as he had been under the Meiji constitution, itself a "constitution granted by the emperor." Instead, he became a "symbol of the state," "deriving his position from the will of the people." In short, this constitution adopted democracy as something that would reinforce Japan's most ancient tradition. It achieved the stunning feat of reaffirming age-old tradition in the name of democracy, and it is possible to see in this cross-breeding of democracy and Japanese tradition a manifestation of postwar Japan's dynamism.

I will have more to say later about political institutions, but I would like to turn now to a brief analysis of how language reflects cultural characteristics. I have discussed this idea more fully in *The Anatomy of Dependence*, in which I argue that the words constituting the nucleus of the concept of *amae* reflect the mentality of the Japanese. Here, I would simply like to note that the hypothesis upon which I based my previous argument is known in linguistics as the Sapir-Whorf hypothesis. I must confess that, though I cited both Sapir and Whorf, I was not aware of the relationship between them when I was writing *The Anatomy of Dependence*, or that both of them based their work on this hypothesis. I discovered this only later, and I want to acknowledge my intellectual debt to them by introducing their work again here.

Sapir's contribution to the hypothesis is summarized in this widely quoted passage:

> Human beings do not live in the objective world alone, nor alone in the world of social activity as ordinarily understood, but are very much at the mercy of the particular language which has become the medium of expression for their society. It is quite an illusion to imagine that one adjusts to reality essentially without the use of language and that language is merely an incidental means of solving specific problems of communication or reflection. The fact of the matter is that the "real world" is to a large extent unconsciously built up on the language habits of the group. . . . We see and hear and otherwise experience very largely as we do because the language habits of our community predispose certain choices of interpretation.[7]

Whorf's work is based on the following, no less widely quoted argument:

> Actually, thinking is most mysterious, and by far the greatest light upon it that we have is thrown by the study of language. This study shows that the forms of a person's thoughts are controlled by inexorable laws of pattern of which he is unconscious. These patterns are the unperceived intricate systematizations of his own language—shown readily enough by a candid

comparison and contrast with other languages, especially those of a different linguistic family. His thinking itself is in a language—in English, in Sanskrit, in Chinese. And every language is a vast pattern-system, different from others, in which are culturally ordained the forms and categories by which the personality not only communicates, but also analyzes nature, notices or neglects types of relationship and phenomena, channels his reasoning, and builds the house of his consciousness.[8]

Above, we considered the concepts of institutions and the individual by positing that they were analogous to those of *tatemae* and *honne*. We have observed how institutions, as the *omote* of a society, express the characteristic cultural features of that society in the two cases of political institutions and language. Next, I would like to examine how the individual, seen as the *ura* of society, is related to these cultural characteristics.

To the extent that the individual, as *ura*, is expressed by *omote* institutions, these institutions also belong to the individual. At the same time, we must also recognize that the individual also possesses something that cannot be expressed by institutions.

In this connection, I would like to refer to the work of Colin Morris, the historian, who argues that the importance of the individual was generally recognized in the West only after the beginning of the twelfth century, and that until that time, the word *individuum* itself did not have the meaning it has today.[9] What Morris so aptly calls the "discovery of the individual" occurred, he suggests, because of massive and rapid social change during this period. No longer able to seek behavioral norms outside of themselves, people in the West began to privilege personal experience. The dynamism generated by this shift of values provided the impetus for the Reformation, the Renaissance, and the Age of Enlightenment, and later for the birth of the United States and the French Revolution. The nineteenth century was the golden age of individualism. But the turn of the twentieth century witnessed the rise of socialism, opposed to individualism, and the competition between these two forces has now developed into a struggle between the superpowers for world domination.

In terms of the distinction between institutions and the individual, however, it is important to note that the historical changes described above have to do with institutions, not with people as individuals, though individuals are of course involved in them. We may speak of individualism, but we are really talking about an institution called individualism, and not about individuals in opposition to that institution. It is an unavoidable conclusion that, even in an individualistic society, the actual individual, as the *ura* of that society, exists in a place that cannot be readily discerned.

Let us examine this conclusion further in light of our comparison between Japan and the United States. It is usual to say that the Japanese are characterized by "group-ism," while Americans are individualistic. I think this is true. The problem, however, is that of the actual position of the individual in the two societies. I would like first to examine this question in the Japanese context of "group-ism."

Japanese are less eager to state personal opinions than to form a consensus. This is reflected, for example, in the unique system of *ringisei*. Closely related to *nemawashi*, *ringisei* is a method of conducting meetings in which achieving a consensus is more important than "winning points."[10] For a Japanese, what group one belongs to is always important, and once one belongs to a group it is virtually impossible to extricate oneself from it. It is because this is true that the Japanese place so much value on *tatemae*. It is not true, however, that Japanese are totally devoted to the group with no concern for individuals.

This is demonstrated by the fact that the word *honne* is so widely used. Just as *honne* exists behind *tatemae*, the individual, in principle, exists in and under the shelter of the group. It is undeniable, of course, that the Japanese consciousness of the individual has been greatly strengthened under the influence of postwar American individualism. But even the most casual reading of Japanese literature will reveal that there was an acute consciousness of the self as individual long before the postwar period—even before the age of Westernization that began with the Meiji Restoration in 1868.

In this context, it is interesting to consider the meanings of *amaeru* in classical Japanese, in which the verb is *amayu*. One meaning of *amayu* is "to become familiar and intimate." But the old word also has the meanings of "to be shy" or "to be self-conscious" (*tereru* in modern Japanese) and "to be bashful and shy" (*hazukashigaru*). I explained in the previous chapter that *amae* is the psychology underlying Japanese group-ism. As is implied by the nuances of *amayu*, however, it is also an extremely personal, individual psychology. It is no exaggeration to suggest that, for the Japanese, awareness of the self as an individual, through *amae*, is actually very much within reach, even though the individual does not seem to emerge on the surface.

Finally, it must not be forgotten that group-ism has always coexisted in Japan with admiration for the great exploit, the lone samurai challenging an opposing army's general, or the rags-to-riches story of the great entrepreneur. It is by no means true that independent action transcending the group is always denied.

Let us next consider American individualism. Americans believe firmly that their system was created for the profit of the individual. To the extent that the principles of self-determination and self-autonomy are institutionally guaranteed, it is unmistakable that there is something quite firm in their individualistic consciousness. And because this is true, even though they are involved in constant cutthroat competition, Americans do not openly display feelings of jealousy and envy, or attempt to trip others up behind their backs. In this way they are quite impressive, and quite unlike the Japanese. But this does not mean that everything about Americans is so impressive. Even if their credulous naivete may sometimes be a virtue, their tendency to be self-righteous is another matter, as is their uniquely American conformism and their surprising tolerance for violent tendencies. One is also given pause by the boom in divorces and the so-called sexual revolution.[11]

All of this can be explained by the following interpretation. For Americans, the *tatemae* is that institutions (the system) and the individual are not contradictory. In other words, their *tatemae* is that there is no distinction between *tatemae* and *honne*. For them, self-determination is the societal rule. Consequently, *honne*, which does not enter into that framework, and of which, therefore, they are unaware, operates in the shadows, producing distortions in self-determination and giving rise to excesses. It is indeed uncanny that in a country where so much weight is put on individuality the most profound demands of the individual are not perceived. And in my opinion, though the word does not exist in English, the name of this most profound demand—the concealed *honne* of which they are unaware—is *amae*. In short, even in a society in which individuals stand out, the appearance of real individuals is strangely absent.

Notes

1. *Nemawashi* 根回し is much more complex than this brief description suggests. The term itself refers to a technique of transplanting trees in traditional Japanese gardening, in which the roots are cut gradually over a period of time so that the tree does not die. Similarly, *nemawashi* in decision-making emphasizes careful and time-consuming negotiations before a proposal is introduced or a final decision is announced.

2. Kyōgoku Junichi, *Nihon no Seiji* [Japanese Politics] (Tokyo: Tokyo University Press, 1983), 160, 253.

3. Charles Horton Cooley, "Institutions and the Person," in *Sociological Theory*, E. F. Borgatta and H. J. Meyer, eds. (New York: Alfred A. Knopf, 1956), 252.

4. In Henry Steele Commager, ed., *Documents of American History* (New York: Appleton-Century-Crofts, Inc., 1958), 100.

5. Alexis de Tocqueville, *Democracy in America* (New York: Vintage Books, 1955), II:349–352.

6. *Constitution of Japan*, in Nobutake Ike, *Japanese Politics* (New York: Alfred A. Knopf, 1957).

7. Edward Sapir, quoted in "The Relation of Habitual Thought and Behavior to Language," in Benjamin Lee Whorf, *Language, Thought, and Reality: Selected Writings of Benjamin Lee Whorf* (Boston: Massachusetts Institute of Technology, 1965), 134.

8. Benjamin Lee Whorf, *Language, Thought and Reality*, 252.

9. Colin Morris, *The Discovery of the Individual*, 1050–1200 (London: S.P.C.K., 1972).

10. *Ringisei* 稟議制 is receiving a great deal of attention from foreigners interested in Japanese-style management. The special feature most often pointed out by foreign observers is that discussion proceeds gradually from the most junior to the most senior participant, whose role, at least in principle (*tatemae*), is simply to formulate the consensus that has emerged.

11. Wagatsuma Hiroshi, *Sei no Jikken: Hendō suru Amerika Bunka* [The Experiment in Sex: Changing American Culture] (Tokyo: Bungei Shunju, 1980); *Kazoku no Hōkai* [The Collapse of the Family] (Tokyo: Bungei Shunju, 1985).

PART TWO

HUMAN BEINGS
IN SOCIETY

Chapter Four

Modes of Human Relations

I stated above that Japanese conduct human relations on the basis of the dual structure of *tatemae* and *honne*. In fact, there may be reason to believe that social life everywhere, not only in Japan, is conducted according to the same kinds of rules. Ultimately, an explanation of Japanese social relations in terms of this dual structure may be possible only because the two words *tatemae* and *honne* exist in the Japanese language. Similarly, I suggested earlier that one of the salient features of this structure is a sense of equilibrium, that it is effective in maintaining psychic balance. However, it must be noted that, precisely to the extent that it is effective in this way, the dual structure of *tatemae* and *honne* is not always easy to command. And, as I also stated above, when the individual fails to master it, social relations become distorted and, indeed, quite difficult.

The writer Natsume Sōseki (1867–1916), in the famous opening passage of his *Kusamakura* (Grass Pillow), provides a good example:

> If one works with his intellect, one's horns show. If one poles his boat with human feeling, one is swept away in the current. If one insists on his pride, one is

confined. In any case, to dwell in the world of human beings is not an easy thing.[1]

The first-person narrator and central character of the novel is talking about the ordeal of getting through life. Japanese respond immediately to this passage, perhaps because every Japanese has experienced difficulty with the dual structure of *tatemae* and *honne*. The hero continues:

When the difficulty of living in the world grows unbearable, one longs to move to a more comfortable place. When one realizes that wherever he might move, it will still be hard to live there, it is then that poems are born, and pictures.[2]

The hero of the novel can say this because he is an artist and a poet. But it is not so easy for most people to become poets, no matter how trying it becomes for them to live in modern society. Consequently, when they are unable to make effective use of *tatemae* and *honne*, they find themselves at a loss.

I would like to explore this problem in concrete terms. First, let us consider the case of an individual who has not learned how to use *tatemae* and attempts to go through life with *honne* alone. Again, Sōseki provides an excellent case study in the central character of *Botchan*.[3] Known and loved by millions of Japanese readers, Botchan seems to me a peerless specimen of the individual who is literally all *honne*.

Botchan confesses to having been a headstrong, naughty child and tells us that he was not loved by his parents. Moreover, his mother's death had been a very traumatic experience. She had died while he was staying with relatives, having been sent away from home as punishment for hurting himself while roughhousing in the kitchen. It was his mother who had scolded him, and she who had sent him away, with the parting words, (translated into English literally) "I don't want to see the face of someone like you." Botchan also tells us that his older brother had blamed him for hastening their mother's death. Throughout all of this, only Kiyo, the family maid, had taken his side. But even though Kiyo had doted on him and indulged him in everything, Botchan claims not to have found this very pleasant.

With this kind of upbringing, Botchan's early life could not have been without difficulty, but he manages somehow and as the story opens, he has finished college and found a job. It is after finishing his education and entering society that Botchan's real problems begin. The novel presents these problems as they arise, in rapid succession, during the month after his arrival in the provincial city where he has reluctantly accepted a teaching position as a middle school mathematics instructor.

On his very first night in Shikoku, he is oversensitive to the treatment he receives at his inn, misinterpreting the well-intentioned remarks of the maids as condescension, and ends up using a third of his meager funds on an exorbitant tip—which really does make him look ridiculous. In his first meeting with the headmaster of the school the next morning, he assumes a haughty, affected attitude, and when the headmaster admonishes him to be a model for the students, he tries to return his letter of appointment, proclaiming, "I cannot fulfill your expectations." He finds it even more irritating when he is expected to greet the other members of the faculty by standing before them one by one with his head bowed, and his appointment letter extended for their perusal. Then, classes begin. With no idea how to deal with middle school students, he loses his composure in the classroom constantly, and soon becomes the butt of the students' jokes and pranks. At his boarding house, he is irritated by everything his landlord says or does and, incapable of making even an attempt to get along with him, ends up getting thrown out.

Botchan fails in one social situation after the other, because he behaves with complete disregard for *tatemae*. In this sense, he is exactly like a child, which is precisely why he is called Botchan. He describes his own personality in the following passage:

> I tried asking the other teachers about it, and they said that for anywhere between a week and a month after receiving their appointments they worried a lot about whether their reputations would turn out good or bad. But I didn't feel that way at all. When I made an occasional mistake in the classroom, I felt bad at the time, but the feeling would disappear completely in thirty minutes or so. I'm the type of guy who can't worry about anything for very long, even if it occurred to me to worry. I was completely indifferent to the influence my mistakes in the classroom might have on the students, and to the reaction that this influence might elicit from the headmaster and his assistant. As I said before, I'm not one of those guys with iron nerves, but I can be very determined once my mind's made up. If things didn't work out at this school I was prepared to go someplace else, so I wasn't scared in the least of either Badger or Redshirt. And I certainly couldn't bring myself to use charm or flattery on the brats in my classes.[4]

In short, Botchan claims to be completely indifferent to his own failure. This may be quite all right for Botchan himself. The problem is that there are situations in which he is not the only person involved. When Redshirt, the headmaster's assistant, warns him against associating with Yamaarashi, the most popular teacher at the school, and hints that Yamaarashi may have instigated the students' pranks, Botchan hurls defiance at him, blustering out, "I'll be O.K. if *I* don't do anything wrong, right?" He becomes even more annoyed when Redshirt laughs at this remark, as if he had said something naive and funny. But in the end he is completely taken in by Redshirt's slanderous insinuations. He begins to have doubts about Yamaarashi and finally picks a quarrel with his former friend. Although he is soon made to realize his mistake and renews his alliance with Yamaarashi, Redshirt skillfully maneuvers him into another trap, and Botchan and Yamaarashi become embroiled in a fight between the middle school students and their rivals from the normal school. Slandered by the local newspapers, they are both forced to resign. Of course, it is intensely satisfying when they succeed in meting out their just revenge on Redshirt and his cohorts, but Botchan must still resign after less than one month at the school, and his friend also loses his job. This can only be called a defeat for Botchan's side.

Sōseki's *Botchan* suggests that a person who has not mastered *tatemae*, no matter how much he or she brandishes *honne*, cannot even protect the all-important self. However, if one cannot dispense with *tatemae*, it is also impossible to conclude that everything will go well if one only observes *tatemae*. In order to explain this in concrete terms, I would like to consider another Japanese literary work, Mori Ōgai's (1831–1907) *Abe Ichizoku* (The Abe Family). Based on historical fact, this short story takes as its theme the feudal custom of *junshi* (following one's lord in death) and depicts the tragic fate of Abe Yaichiemon Michinobu and his family when they run afoul of the *tatemae* of this custom. The narrator of the story describes the custom in the following passage:

> When or why they had become established is not clear, but there were naturally rules for *junshi*. However much one held one's lord dear, it was not something that anyone could do on his own initiative.

It was the same thing as accompanying one's lord on his attendance in Edo in this age of the great peace, or accompanying him on the battlefield in times of war. In order to follow one's lord on his journey to Mount Shide and the Sanzu River, it was absolutely essential to have his permission. To die without his assent was to die a dog's death.[5]

Before his death, Hosokawa Tadatoshi (1584–1641), lord of the Higo Kumamoto realm, formally assented to the *junshi* of eighteen personal retainers. However, Abe Yaichiemon Michinobu, one of the retainers whose position made it natural that he should commit *junshi*, was denied permission, forcing him and his entire family onto a path toward inexorable destruction.

What is important here is the problem of why Yaichiemon could not obtain Tadatoshi's assent, but before entering that discussion, consider the following passage, which describes the mental state of Naitō Chōjūrō Mototsugu, one of the eighteen retainers who were given permission to commit *junshi*:

Chōjūrō was still a callow youth with not a single outstanding act of meritorious service to his credit, but Tadatoshi had shown him favor from the very beginning and had always used him near his own person. A hard drinker, Chōjūrō had also committed blunders of etiquette for which another person would have been reprimanded, but Tadatoshi would just laugh and say, "Chōjūrō didn't do it, the *saké* did."

Convinced that he must repay this debt of gratitude [*on*[6]] and make amends for his mistakes, Chōjūrō came to believe firmly that there was no other path to requital and atonement than to follow his lord in death. But if we enter this man's heart [*kokoro*] and examine it more closely, besides the feeling that he must follow his lord on his own initiative, there existed with almost equal strength the feeling that, since people no doubt thought of him as one of the retainers who should naturally do so, he had no choice but to die. It felt as if he were relying on other people as he progressed toward his own death. But on the other hand again he was worried that if he did not follow Tadatoshi in death he would certainly undergo horrible humiliation at the hands of others.[7]

From this, we understand that Chōjūrō's mental state is extremely complex, that his *tatemae* and his *honne* are subtly shifting back and forth. Moreover, Chōjūrō's story is told in some detail, and it is clear that, for the author Ōgai, he is representative of the eighteen retainers who are permitted to commit *junshi*. But Tadatoshi's mental state is equally complex, with the same subtle shifts from *tatemae* to *honne*, as we learn in the following:

Among the retainers who had long received favor, there were eighteen people, including Chōjūrō, who each in his own way requested and received permission around this time to follow their lord in death, just as Chōjūrō had held Tadatoshi's feet and begged for his consent. All of them were deeply trusted retainers. Therefore, in his own mind [*kokoro*], Tadatoshi would very much like to have left these men behind to protect his heir, Mitsuhisa. Moreover, he duly felt the cruelty of allowing them to accompany him in death. And yet it had been inevitable that, even as he felt his heart break, he should give to each of them that single word, permitted.

Tadatoshi believed that these men, his most intimate retainers, did not begrudge him their lives. And he knew also that self-immolation would therefore hold no pain for them. Against this, how would things be if he left them without permission to follow him in death and they lived on after him? The entire clan would consider them people who had failed to die when they should have. They would be looked upon as people who knew no gratitude [*on*], as craven cowards, whose age and experience were no longer worthy of respect. If that were all, they would perhaps endure the humiliation and wait for the time to come when they could offer up their lives to his son Mitsuhisa. But they would not be able to bear it if there were those who said that the previous lord had unwittingly used these ungrateful cowards in his own service. What feelings of mortification they might suffer. When he thought of this, Tadatoshi had felt compelled to say, "It is permitted." When the number of retainers granted permission to die with him reached eighteen, Tadatoshi, who for more than fifty years had played his role both in times of peace and times of turbulence, and who had been through personal and worldly affairs to the point of weariness, pondered deeply, even in the pain of his illness, on his own death and the deaths of these eighteen samurai. That which has life must certainly perish. Beside the old tree, withered and dying, the young tree rises up dense with foliage. From the standpoint of the young officers surrounding Mitsuhisa, his heir, it would be better if the old retainers Tadatoshi had appointed himself were not there. They were in the way. He wished that they could give to Mitsuhisa the same service they had given him, but already there were others who were prepared to serve Mitsuhisa, others who might well be waiting impatiently. The people he had appointed had no doubt incurred enmity in fulfilling their respective duties over the years. They at least must have been the objects of envy. Perhaps it would not have been wise to order them to live on after him. Perhaps it had been merciful to give them permission to follow him. With these thoughts, Tadatoshi felt that he had gained a measure of solace.[8]

Together, these passages make it clear that there is a mentality at work here that is implicitly shared by the retainers, who must beg to follow him in death, and Tadatoshi, who must reluctantly give his permission. Moreover, it is precisely because this is true that they are given permission to commit *junshi*. In the case of Yaichiemon, the problem is that this kind of mutual relationship had not been established. Instead, the narrator tells us, "The fact is that Tadatoshi had fallen into the contrary habit of refusing to listen to anything Yaichiemon had to say." Ōgai develops his interpretation of this difficult relationship more fully in the following:

Yaichiemon would do things on his own initiative that other people would do only if they were told to do so. What other people would do only after informing Tadatoshi, Yaichiemon would do without informing him. However, what he did always went right to the heart of the matter, and he was above criticism. Gradually, Yaichiemon had begun to serve from pride alone. At first, Tadatoshi had thought nothing of it. It was just that whenever he saw this man's face, he wanted to oppose him. It had been later, when he learned that Yaichiemon was serving from his own pride, that he had come to think him hateful. But even though he hated him, the wise Tadatoshi reflected on why Yaichiemon had become this way, and realized that he himself was the cause. He had thought to mend his habit of always opposing Yaichiemon, but as the months and then the years accumulated it became increasingly difficult to do so.[9]

It is as if Tadatoshi secretly felt satisfaction in opposing Yaichiemon, and Yaichiemon, for his part, tacitly assented to this and served him all the more faithfully. But Tadatoshi's whims are not the only factor in the development of this relationship, for Yaichiemon also has his contrary habits.

For any person, there is someone beloved above all others, and another who is most detested. When one delves into why one person is beloved and the other hateful, there is nothing to rely on that might enable one to grasp it. Tadatoshi's dislike of Yaichiemon was of this nature. However, it is beyond doubt that there was something about Yaichiemon that made it difficult to get close to him. We know this to be true, for he had few intimate friends. Everyone respected him as a brilliant samurai. But there was no one who attempted to approach him lightly. Even if someone occasionally tried to get close to him out of curiosity, that person would soon lose patience and become estranged from Yaichiemon. In the period when Yaichiemon was still called Inosuke, and still had his forelocks, an older man who had occasionally struck up a conversation or lent him a hand with something finally gave up, conceding, 'There are no chinks in Abe to get through to him.' Considering this, there is nothing strange about the fact that, even though he wanted to, Tadatoshi could not correct his habit of opposing Yaichiemon.[10]

The older man who says that "there are no chinks in Abe to get through to him" could have said that "he doesn't reveal his faults," or that "he doesn't reveal his *honne*." In other words, everything Yaichiemon says or does is strictly according to *tatemae*. He is a stickler. In English slang, he would be called a "square." People who had daily contact with him must have felt that he gave them no breathing space, and he was undoubtedly difficult to deal with. It is by no means unreasonable that Tadatoshi should have disliked him. But, for Yaichiemon, Tadatoshi's refusal to grant him permission to commit *junshi* was a fatal blow. To vindicate his honor, he is forced to commit *seppuku* in a grotesquely brutal manner, but this in no way wipes away his humiliation, and instead leads to tragedy for his family. His sons inherit his disgrace and are finally forced into a confrontation with Tadatoshi's heir that ends in the destruction of the entire Abe family. Of course, this is a story about the distant past, and could never occur today. Nevertheless, it is as true now as it was then that one cannot get through life successfully by insisting on *tatemae* alone.

As we have seen in the examples of Sōseki's *Botchan* and Ōgai's *Abe Ichizoku*, neither *tatemae* or *honne* is effective as a single guiding principle. But people like Botchan and Yaichiemon are at least able to make some sort of distinction between the two. They may be difficult people to deal with, but they are never actually frightening. However, a person who has become an adult without learning to make this distinction will be psychically defeated by the slightest setback, and may be truly difficult to handle. This is true of many patients who need psychiatric help.

I wanted to avoid using case studies of real people to illustrate this problem, so I tried looking around for a character in literature. Within the scope of my own knowledge, I could not find such a character in Japanese literature. I decided, therefore, to use *King Lear* as an example. To be sure, *King*

Lear is from the Western literary tradition, and it is an extremely difficult text. My attempt to interpret it by applying the Japanese concepts of *tatemae* and *honne* may well be attacked as preposterous. I feel, however, that if this interpretation makes *King Lear* easier to understand than before, it will demonstrate that there is at least that much universality in the concepts of *tatemae* and *honne*.

What is relevant to my argument here is the famous opening scene, in which the aging Lear, having decided to divide his kingdom among his three daughters, summons them to the inheritance ceremony and asks which of them loves him most. This is the most decisive scene in the construction of the drama, for it is here that Cordelia is banished and that Lear entrusts his kingdom to Goneril and Regan, who will later conspire to betray him and bring about his death. But why does Cordelia drive her father into such a rage? Consider the scene. Goneril and Regan have exhausted words, eloquently proclaiming that they love Lear above everyone else. Cordelia is commanded to speak, setting the stage for the following:

> Cordelia: Nothing, my lord.
>
> Lear: Nothing!
>
> Cordelia: Nothing.
>
> Lear: Nothing will come of nothing.
>   Speak again.
>
> Cordelia: Unhappy that I am, I cannot heave
>   My heart into my mouth. I love your Majesty
>   According to my bond; no more nor less.
>
> Lear: How, how, Cordelia! Mend your speech a little,
>   Lest you may mar your fortunes.

Cordelia: Good my lord,
    You have begot me, bred me, lov'd me; I
    Return those duties back as are right fit,
    Obey you, love you, and most honour you.
    Why have my sisters husbands, if they say
    They love you all? Haply, when I shall wed,
    That lord whose hand must take my plight
        shall carry
    Half my love with him, half my care and duty.
    Sure I shall never marry like my sisters,
    To love my father all.[11]

Clearly, Cordelia is strongly conscious of her older sisters. Indeed, it is as if she answered her father in this way in order to strike back at them. Instead of replying to her father's demand, she is intent throughout on criticizing her sisters.

In terms of *tatemae* and *honne*, the two older sisters say the lines of the *tatemae* that is appropriate in this situation, while Cordelia attempts to express her own true *honne*. But by doing so she goes against the will of her father, who had intended this to be the occasion for giving her his blessing and choosing between her two suitors the most appropriate husband for her. He has already decided to abdicate his throne and divide his kingdom among his three daughters. Since Cordelia is his favorite, she not only could have avoided exile, but also could have won "a share more opulent than her sisters" by simply making her father happy. Conscious only of her sisters, however, she fails completely to consider Lear's feelings.

But even if Cordelia is partly to blame, we are still left with the question of why Lear failed to comprehend her true intentions (*kokoro*). He is also unable to see the true motives beneath the eloquent, but insincere, protestations of love by Goneril and Regan. It can only be said that Lear is incapable of reading the *kokoro* that exists in the *ura* of words. He does not understand the distinction between words and intention (*kokoro*); or, in other words, the distinction between *tatemae* and *honne*. Perhaps this is because he has been enfeebled with age, but I think it is closer to the mark to suggest that, in his long years as king, he has grown accustomed to having people follow his orders. He has never learned that every human being has *tatemae* and *ura*. And he must go through unspeakable torments in the rest of the play before he finally does learn.

After abdicating his throne, Lear experiences his world crashing down around him. He falls into a state of raving madness, but finally is able to see the truth. Of course, had he demonstrated even a little wisdom from the very beginning, the situation would never have come to this. Even if he had been displeased with Cordelia's answer, he would not have had to go so far as to banish her, and he still would have been able to live with each of his daughters in turn, just as he had planned. Though he might still have experienced some discomfort and dissatisfaction, at least Cordelia's home would have been more comfortable than those of her sisters, and Goneril and Regan could not have treated him so unkindly in her presence.

The play is virtually an allegory. In order to live out his old age in comfort, Lear would have had to make his daughters coexist, and to do so, he would have had to make careful distinctions between *tatemae* and *honne*. Moreover, he would have to have understood that both *tatemae* and *honne* function as dual principles. This is what the story of King Lear suggests to me. And I am convinced that such a reading of the play is by no means farfetched, for the delicate psychic balance that Lear failed to achieve between *tatemae* and *honne* is the very balance that we seek today in our relations with others.

Notes

1. Natsume Sōseki, *Kusamakura*, in *Sōseki Zenshū* [The Collected Works of Natsume Sōseki] (Tokyo: Iwanami Shoten, 1966), 2:387. [For a complete

English translation, see Alan Turney, trans., *The Three-Cornered World*, (Peter Owen, 1975; Tokyo: Tuttle, 1966; Chicago: Henry Regnery, 1967). *Kusamakura* was first published in 1906.—Trans.]

2. Ibid.

3. Natsume Sōseki, *Botchan*, in *Sōseki Zenshū*, 2:241–383. [For a complete English translation, see Alan Turney, trans., *Botchan* (Tokyo: Kodansha International, 1972; London: Peter Owen, 1973). *Botchan* is a term of endearment for young boys. Often, as in Sōseki's novel, it is used by servants and has the meaning of "little master," or "young master." When it is applied by an outsider to someone who has reached the age of the novel's central character, however, it has the connotation of "a young man who has not grown up yet." *Botchan* was first published in 1906.—Trans.]

4. Ibid., 265.

5. Mori Ōgai, *Abe Ichizoku*, in *Mori Ōgai Shū* (Tokyo: Shinchōsha, 1971), 351. [For a complete English translation, see David Dilworth, trans., "The Abe Family," in *The Incident at Sakai, and Other Stories* (Honolulu: University Press of Hawaii, 1977), 37–69. *Abe Ichizoku* was first published in 1913.—Trans.]

6. *On* 恩 and *giri* 義理, a closely related concept, were part of the neo-Confucian ethical code, which dominated the Edo period and still makes its appearance in modern human relations. *On* refers to debts of personal gratitude, while *giri* refers to specific obligations implicit in a relationship. In this case, for example, Chōjūrō and Tadatoshi both have specific obligations (*giri*) to each other as lord and retainer, but Chōjūrō owes a debt of gratitude (*on*) to Tadatoshi for his personal favor. In this sense, *giri* belongs to *omote* and *tatemae* while *on* belongs to *ura* and *honne*. I have also considered *on* and *giri* from the perspective of *amae* in *The Anatomy of Dependence* and *The Psychological World of Natsume Sōseki*. See also "*Giri-Ninjō*: An Interpretation," in *Aspects of Social Change*, R. P. Dore, ed. (Princeton, New Jersey: Princeton University Press, 1967).

7. *Abe Ichizoku*, 352.

8. Ibid., 354.

9. Ibid., 358.

10. Ibid., 358–359.

11. *King Lear*, act 1, sc. 1, lines 86–102. [Citations of Shakespeare's plays are from Peter Alexander, ed., *The Complete Works of William Shakespeare* (London and Glasgow: Collins, 1985).—Trans.]

Chapter Five

Human Beings Stripped Naked

In my explanation of the concepts of *tatemae* and *honne*, I mentioned that we often imply by our use of these words that the opposition between *tatemae* and *honne* is hierarchical: that *tatemae* is directed at *omote*, and therefore false, and that only *honne* represents the real truth. There are many other expressions that suggest this hierarchy: "That is nothing but the *tatemae*" or "It won't do any good to keep talking about the *tatemae*." We are more anxious to learn the *honne* of a situation than the *tatemae*, and this is an expression of the same feeling that *honne* is the natural state, while *tatemae* is an "unnatural complication." The fact that we no longer place much weight on ceremony, that the words "formal" and "formalism" almost always contain critical nuances, is a reflection of the same modern tendency.

In Japan, this privileging of *honne* and its opposite, depreciation of *tatemae*, became a conspicuous social phenomenon only after World War Two, but some far-sighted thinkers seem to have perceived omens of such a development much earlier. For example, among the works he published during the war, I have discovered a *zuihitsu* (discursive essay) by the critic Kobayashi Hideo (1902–1983) that touches on just this theme. It records his impressions on an occasion when he had gone to see a Nō performance. Drawn by the mysterious charm of the Nō mask, he turned away from the stage to look over the faces in the audience. But he found not even one that was so captivating that he could not draw his eyes away. After stating that all of the expressions looming out from the audience were restless and bored, Kobayashi makes this comment on modern civilization:

> Strip off the mask and look at the naked face!—this thing called modern civilization seems to shriek nothing but such nonsense, as it rushes ahead not knowing where it is going. Rousseau did not confess or repent a single thing in his *Les Confessions*. Is it not rather the effeminate malice that he scattered about so lavishly throughout that book, and of which neither he nor his readers were aware, that has gradually spread without end? Throughout the *Kyōgen* performance, I felt vaguely that I was being pursued in a nightmare.[1]

The problem Kobayashi addresses in observing this contrast between the mask and the bare face corresponds to the problem I am dealing with in this book: the relationship between *omote* and *ura*, and between *tatemae* and *honne*. Since we hide our real faces with masks, does it follow that a splendid face will emerge if only we strip away the mask? Kobayashi's answer is no, the same answer suggested by my argument that it is not always, or even usually true, that things go well if only *honne*, stripped of *tatemae*, is allowed to emerge. I say this because *honne*, by its very nature, hangs in the framework of *tatemae*: without *tatemae*, one cannot have *honne*. Or, returning to the metaphor suggested by Kobayashi's essay, since it is *honne* that performs *tatemae*, if the *tatemae* is bad, then the *honne* that performs it is bad. We must conclude, therefore, that there is no reason for us to believe that if only we strip away the *tatemae* a better *honne* will necessarily emerge from behind it.

Kobayashi suggests that the trend toward the privileging of "real faces" began with modern civilization. The philosopher Sakabe Megumi goes even further. In a recent work, entitled *Kamen no Kaishakugaku* (The Hermeneutics of Masks), Sakabe points out that it is a "special modern phenomenon" to believe that it is the bare face that is the reality of human beings, and that a mask is something put on from outside the human being.[2] Even if it is true that the privileging of *honne* became a conspicuous social phenomenon only after World War Two, it is worth noting that, much earlier, the writer Natsume Sōseki had created in *Botchan* a character who personified that tendency.

According to Kobayashi, the appearance of this tendency in the West is related to Rousseau. Again, however, it may have begun much earlier. Shakespeare's *King Lear* was written at the beginning of the seventeenth century, and as we have seen, the main characters of the play all have an extreme tendency to despise *tatemae*. Goneril, Regan, and Edmund reveal this attitude when they pretend to construct a *tatemae* and then betray it, but such characters have existed throughout the ages, and it would probably be mistaken to see them as particularly modern. But Cordelia, who considers *tatemae* to be nothing more than pretense and attempts to proceed without it, is very clearly modern. On this point she resembles Botchan. Lear, for his part, expects to be treated as a king even after divesting himself of his royal privileges, and in this he is ignoring *tatemae*. He too can perhaps be called modern. Interestingly, among Shakespeare's plays, *King Lear* was poorly received for a very long period. Indeed, it was not until after the middle of this century that its true value was recognized. One may well wonder if this was not because its modernism was far ahead of its time.

Lear, Cordelia, and Botchan all suffer painful blows, blows

to which they are subjected precisely because they ignore *tatemae*. I have suggested that, in this sense, they anticipate the modern age. It is interesting that the fool makes fun of Lear for having renounced his rights by saying, "All thy other titles thou hast given away; that thou wast born with."[3] A modern reader does not need the loyal Kent's warning that "this is not altogether fool." Lear has become quite literally a naked king, a point which never fails to remind me of Andersen's famous story, *The Emperor's New Clothes*.

The emperor in Andersen's story is fond of always wearing new clothes. He is duped by a swindler, who assures him that his are the finest garments in the world—so splendid, in fact, that fools and the low born cannot even see them. With the help of the swindler, the emperor dons this wonderful raiment, and then embarks on a procession through the town, stark naked. At first, the townspeople seem to actually see the invisible clothes, but a child suddenly shouts, "He is not wearing anything!" Then, everyone realizes that the emperor is naked.

This is scathing satire, exposing the folly of royalty who believe that majesty resides in their own bodies. Naked, even an emperor is only a person. In more general, abstract terms, the emperor's nakedness is *ura* without the cover of *omote*, *honne* that has lost the frame of *tatemae*, the individual unprotected by institutions. And, moreover, it is a statement that if one of the elements of these oppositions is excluded, it is certain that the other will also be useless.

Let us return to *King Lear* to examine these points in terms of the interior aspect of the psyche. When, by Goneril's own words, the unsuspecting Lear is made to realize her betrayal, he doubts his own eyes, and asks, "Are you our daughter?" And then, in his anguish and his wrath, shouts the following lines: "Does any here know me? This is not Lear. Does Lear walk thus? speak thus? Where are his eyes? . . . Who is it that can tell me who I am?"[4]

His world crumbling away beneath his feet, he no longer understands who he himself is, and he bears this anguish until his death at the end of the play. In modern terms, Lear has been thrown into an identity crisis.

The Japanese translation of "identity" (*dōitsusei*) is not very familiar to most people. It contains two meanings: to identify with someone or something (*dōitsuka*), and to identify something as such (*dōtei*). The former refers to the binding of oneself to another (thing or person), and the latter to identifying a thing as that thing. Simply put, identity is to be aware of oneself as oneself. But its significance as a technical concept lies in the suggestion that this awareness of self is constituted on the basis of connections with others. In the case of Lear, this is most clearly indicated by the fact that Lear begins to feel that he is no longer himself in the very instant he is made to realize that his relationship with his daughter is no longer what it had been in the past.

The word identity was first used in its psychological sense by Erik H. Erikson in seminal research published immediately after World War Two. In his use of the term, it refers to both continuity of the self and the self's connection with others.[5] Erikson perceived that an understanding of psychology and pathology in adolescents must proceed from the viewpoint that a person's principal task in adolescence is the formation of an identity. Erikson's work was epoch-making, not only in linking the fields of psychiatry, psychology, anthropology, and sociology, but also in terms of its enormous effect in helping humanity to recognize itself in the modern world.

The devalorization of *tatemae*—indeed, the disregard for *tatemae*—in the contemporary age has reached the point where even institutions that have endured for centuries are being made the objects of skepticism. The consequences of this are that people's sense of belonging has faded and that their sense of social roles has become extremely fluid. Young people, even if they are not particularly ill mentally, can no longer grasp their identities. Even adults who once thought they knew themselves very well are now often placed in situations where they must ask themselves again just who they are. In this way, the word identity has become indispensable for expressing the consciousness of contemporary mankind. Even in Japanese, the English word, only slightly altered by its *katakana* pronunciation, is used almost everyday.[6]

Above, I have suggested that the weakening of *tatemae* has invited an identity crisis in the modern age. Next, and it amounts to the same thing in the end, I would like to say a word about the advent of another extremely paradoxical phenomenon, in which the privileging of *honne*, although it apparently creates hypertrophy in the private world, is in fact an invasion of privacy. This phenomenon occurs because personal privacy is privacy only when it is protected by public institutions. Without institutions, privacy, no matter how much it expands, is actually being exposed to the outside and, ultimately, invaded.

Perhaps the most concrete evidence of this is the collapse of the family. Society today is changing violently, and the family has been placed right in the center of this change. It may seem that the family is protected even now, and its economic foundation, at least, has been guaranteed in many of the developed countries. However, in direct proportion to this, the family circle itself is being threatened. People are constantly lured outside the family, and it is no longer easy to relax even within the family setting. The family becomes scattered; its individual members are thrown out into society. But the family is the original basis for nurturing privacy. When its function is undermined, identity and privacy are forced to stand alone. Consider the famous films of Ingmar Bergman—*Wild Strawberries, Autumn Sonata, Scenes from a Marriage*. All of them deal with the tragedy of families in crisis, no doubt because this is the single most salient feature of modern society. Even without citing the example of Bergman, it can be said that much of contemporary literature reflects this current in the modern world.

We can think of the family as the first knot binding together *tatemae* and *honne*. Therefore, it is the collapse of the family that most dramatically indicates a split between them. On this point, it is extremely interesting to note that in the process of a divorce one partner in the marriage will ultimately come to represent *tatemae* while the other represents *honne*. That is, eventually there will be a polarization of *tatemae* and *honne*.

Naturally, both the husband and the wife must have *tatemae* and *honne*. When the couple is in harmony, they both agree at least on the *tatemae* of maintaining the family. But when the harmony of the marriage is compromised, one of them will come to insist completely on his or her *tatemae* and the other will be equally insistent on his or her *honne*. If the marriage finally collapses, it is in many ways the children who receive the greatest injury, for they are deprived of the chance to distinguish the *tatemae* and *honne* within themselves. This loss is semipermanent. If they go out into the world in this condition, their ability to withstand stress will of course be weakened, and they will not be able to escape difficulties.

Yet another special feature of the present age is the increasingly vociferous debate over human rights. This may be generally interpreted as a sign that people have awakened to the importance of human rights due to the progress of civilization. In fact, it is quite the opposite. It is much closer to the truth to think of it as a result of the fact that the steady and accelerating advance of the multifarious ways of invading privacy has strengthened people's sense of crisis.

George Orwell's *Nineteen Eighty-Four*, for example, while most explicitly a warning against totalitarian trends in the modern age, can also be interpreted in a much broader sense as an indictment of the modern age as a whole. In Orwell's world of the future, speech and thought are totally controlled, monitored by devices such as telescreens and hidden microphones. The family has become merely a place for producing children, and bonds of family or personal friendship are strictly prohibited. Any writing that might recall the culture and tradition of the past, including everyday language, has been eradicated. Of course, Orwell's is an extreme view of the future, but no one can deny that the germ of such a society already exists in today's world.

Personally, I am one of those who views the collapse of the family today as the most serious sign of this society of the future that Orwell has drawn. George Steiner, a prominent critic of modern society, suggests that the invasion of privacy is the most characteristic feature of the modern age. Steiner does not deal directly with the collapse of the family as such, but it would in no way be a distortion of Steiner's meaning to substitute the words "family life" for "privacy" in the following passage from his *Language and Silence*.

> Future historians may come to characterize the present era in the West as one of a massive onslaught on human privacy, on the delicate processes by which we seek to become our own singular selves, to hear the echo of our specific being. This onslaught is being pressed by the very conditions of an urban masstechnocracy, by the necessary uniformities of our economic and political choices, by the new electronic media of communication and persuasion, by the everincreasing exposure of our thought and actions to sociological, psychological, and material intrusions and controls. Increasingly, we come to know real privacy, real space in which to experiment with our sensibility, only in extreme guises: nervous breakdown, addiction, economic failure. Hence the appal-

ling monotony and *publicity*—in the full sense of the
word—of so many outwardly prosperous lives.[7]

Steiner suggests that mental illness and other extreme conditions have become spaces in which people experience privacy. I
will have more to say about mental illness in the next chapter,
but here it is necessary to point out that the fundamental
character of mental illness is in fact a loss of inner privacy, and
if this is true, Steiner's interpretation would seem not to be in ac-
cord with the facts. However, this apparent contradiction can
be comprehended if it is understood that mental illness has
characteristics in common with all other illness. For example, a
high fever is a symptom of illness, but at the same time it is also
evidence that the body is resisting by trying to overcome the
virus that has caused the illness. Similarly, the mentally ill have
not only lost their inner privacy, but are also suffering from
that loss. Indeed, it can be said that their suffering is the only
privacy they have left. In this way, their illness, even though it
is an illness, points toward health. In fact, most people understand the true blessing of health only after they become ill. It is
precisely in this sense that Steiner speaks of mental illness as
one of the only spaces in which we experience privacy.

Noteworthy in this connection is the fact that the hero of
Nineteen Eighty-Four, in spite of having been deprived of his
privacy, still struggles desperately to maintain it, and does
manage to experience privacy, if only barely. Of course, we
must also note that after receiving his "therapeutic torture" he
gives up all resistance and becomes a lifeless shell. The original
title of this book, interestingly, was *The Last Man in Europe*,
which hints very strongly at Orwell's true intention in writing
it. It is also extraordinarily fascinating in light of the analysis
above.

I would like to conclude this chapter by saying one final
word about Steiner's *Language and Silence*. Elsewhere in his

book, Steiner suggests that the invasion of privacy is especially characteristic of modern society in Western Europe. While this is certainly true, I think we must also recognize the advent of the same kind of phenomena in other developed countries, of which Japan is the best example. As I pointed out at the beginning of this chapter, it is precisely because this is true that the privileging of *honne* and disregard for *tatemae* have become the dominant trends in contemporary Japanese society.

Despite this fact, however, one still feels that Japan has for some reason maintained a higher degree of stability in comparison with the advanced nations of the West. On the one hand, modernization has proceeded at an extraordinary rate of speed, the old morality is being eroded, and the streets are flooded with pornography and what Steiner calls "sub-erotic" publications and advertising. There is now a great vogue for stripping people naked, both physically and mentally. Nevertheless, crime has not increased to a point where the average citizen fears for life and limb on a daily basis, and the divorce rate, although increasing rapidly, is still much lower than that of developed countries in the West. If one insists on interpreting this as a reflection of the conservative nature of the Japanese, there is nothing more to say. But I wonder if it is not more accurate to say that it is evidence of the Japanese sense of psychic balance. I say this because the Japanese, while they may sometimes react to foreign trends so sensitively as to seem servile and adulating, also seem to manage somehow to maintain their own preferences. In the *omote*, their depriviledging of *tatemae* may be equal to that of Westerners, and they may have fundamental doubts about various institutions, but this is itself the *tatemae* of a new age, and the balance between *tatemae* and *honne* is preserved.

This is related to the fact that, unlike Westerners, Japanese do not think of the individual and the group as being fundamentally in conflict. Japanese group-ism is different from the totalitarianism depicted in *Nineteen Eighty-Four*. It is based on an instinctual sense that the support of the group is indispensable for the individual. Because of this, the Japanese are now performing a tight-rope act, going along with the modern fashion of devalorizing *tatemae* even as they attempt to maintain it.

Notes

1. Kobayashi Hideo, *Taema* [Taema Temple], in *Mujō to iu koto, Mōtsuarto* ["The Thing Called Transience" and "Mozart"], *Kobayashi Hideo Zenshū* [The Complete Works of Kobayashi Hideo] (Tokyo: Shinchōsha, 1983), 15. [Kobayashi Hideo was the founder of modern literary criticism in Japan. Highly influential in introducing modern Western thought, he nevertheless feared that it would be shallowly understood. As is clear from this passage, he had very definite opinions about what he read, and the flow of his writing can be somewhat shocking. Here, his anger at the sight of a Japanese audience that is incapable of appreciating a Nō performance leads to a highly charged discussion of Rousseau.—Trans.]

2. Sakabe Megumi, *Fujita Mitsue no Kotodama-ron* [Fujita Mitsue's Theory of *Kotodama*], in *Kamen no Kaishakugaku* [The Hermeneutics of Masks] (Tokyo: Tokyo University Press, 1979), 211–239, 326.

3. *King Lear*, act 1, sc. 4, lines 148–149.

4. *King Lear*, act 1, sc. 4, lines 224–229.

5. Erik H. Erikson, *Childhood and Society* (New York: W. W. Norton, 1963). See especially "Part Four: Youth and the Evolution of Identity," 277–284.

6. *Katakana* is a phonetic syllabary. In everyday language, it is used almost exclusively for foreign words, of which an enormous, and growing number have entered modern Japanese.

7. George Steiner, "Night Words," in *Language and Silence* (New York: Atheneum, 1967), 76. It is interesting to note that this essay deals with the popularity of pornography in postwar Europe, and that its publication was met by a storm of angry protest.

Chapter Six

Human Beings Split Apart

We have considered a number of situations in which the dual structure of *tatemae* and *honne* breaks down; in which individuals do not, or cannot, manipulate it effectively. Here, I would like to consider one final case, an extreme case in which *tatemae* and *honne* are in such violent conflict that the individual is in danger of being torn apart.

I have suggested that the relationship between *tatemae* and *honne* is symbiotic, that they are mutually constitutive. The case of extreme conflict between them may seem to contradict this analysis. That this contradiction is only apparent, however, can be easily understood, I think, if the reader will consider a situation in which a person wants to do away with *tatemae* for some reason, but is unable to do so. If this person can brazen it out, behaving without regard for anything but personal desires, he or she can get through the situation, even though the person may be accused of "having an *ura-omote*" (being insincere). If the person can do away with the inconvenient *tatemae* by contriving a new one, nothing could be better. The problem, however, is a situation in which the person can do neither, in which a number of *tatemae*, all different in kind, pile up and overlap. With the increasing complexity of modern society, such situations only grow more numerous.

The same person, for example, may belong to two groups that are completely antagonistic. To lean toward one of them is to ignore the other, giving rise to a condition that I describe as *tatemae* and *honne* colliding. Western scholars have also turned their attention to this phenomenon of modern social life, though they do not use the words *tatemae* and *honne*. Among them is the noted psychologist and thinker William James:

> Properly speaking, *a man has as many social selves as there are individuals who recognize him* and carry an image of him in their mind. To wound any one of these images is to wound him. But as the individuals who carry the images fall naturally into classes, we may practically say that he has as many different social selves as there are distinct *groups* of persons about whose opinion he cares. He generally shows a different side of himself to each of these different groups. Many a youth who is demure enough before his parents and teachers, swears and swaggers like a pirate among his "tough" young friends. We do not show ourselves to our children as to our club-companions, to our customers as to the laborers we employ, to our own masters and employers as to our intimate friends. From this there results what practically is a division of the man into several selves; and this may be a discordant splitting, as where one is afraid to let one set of his acquaintances know him as he is elsewhere; or it may be a perfectly harmonious division of labor, as where one tender to his children is stern to the soldiers or prisoners under his control.[1]

It is easy to see that what James describes as a discordant splitting, in which a person's various social selves are mutually divided and in conflict, is first one in which gaps and conflicts exist among the various people with whom the person has relationships. Speaking more generally, G. H. Mead has written that "the unity and structure of the complete self reflects the unity and structure of the social process as a whole."[2] If this is true, then discordant splitting in society amounts to splitting of the human ego. In a sense, that is, when human beings are involved with other people who are in conflict, they take these conflicts into their own selves, internalizing them as conflicts within themselves.

To be sure, as long as the conflicts are not severe, people can manipulate *tatemae* and *honne*, depending on which one of their various relationships they are dealing with. Even in this case, of course, there is a splitting of the ego, but human beings are capable of enduring this splitting to a certain degree. But as the degree of splitting intensifies, the person's identity as an individual will become confused. If it is only a matter of conflict between *omote* and *ura*, or between *tatemae* and *honne*, the person still maintains the appearance of a human being, but when the splits within have become so deep that *omote* and *ura*, and *tatemae* and *honne*, are all mixed up—with only various scenes appearing unrelated to each other in any meaningful order—then identity has been completely destroyed.

Since ancient times, humanity has concentrated enormous effort on devising various ways of averting this final splitting of the human being. First, since this splitting originates in society, we can consider the method of working directly on society itself, striving to eliminate societal splits and conflicts, or at least to reduce them to the lowest possible limit. This would amount to establishing a *tatemae* recognized as widely as possible by the members of a society. But this is no easy task. It usually requires a resort to force, and once things come to this, we are talking about an eminently political problem. In fact, looking back on history from this point of view, human beings have always sought unity and peace. Indeed, so earnest has been this quest that even social splits and conflicts themselves have always occurred in the name of unity and peace.

The Old Testament story of the tower of Babel is highly suggestive in this regard. In an age when all human beings still spoke the same language, humanity sought to flaunt its unity before God by building an impregnable citadel and a great tower reaching up to heaven. But God was displeased, and frustrated their plan by causing their language to be confused and scattering humanity to the far reaches of the earth.

This story illustrates both the ancientness of humanity's aspiration for unity, and the fact that this aspiration has always been doomed to failure. It is a story with much relevance for the modern age, for while we have witnessed the advent of an age in which the world is a single entity, united by technology, political splits are occurring everywhere. Voices calling for unity and peace are louder than ever before, but the language of politics is so confused that it is impossible to tell whether they are crying out for unity and peace because the world is split apart, or whether the world is split apart because of the clamor for unity and peace itself.

Politics may seem a rather large subject. Instead of worrying about the whole world, there may be those who feel it would make more sense to content oneself with reducing splitting in matters closer at hand. As the Confucian classics say: "Cultivate the self, harmonize the family, govern the country, and then pacify the world." Certainly, this would seem to be the natural order. But things are not always so easy. Whether in the case of an individual or a group, internal unity (internal bonding) often can be achieved by having external enemies or by making everything bad the fault of conditions or persons outside. In effect, this would mean virtually severing all external relations. But this is becoming increasingly difficult in the modern world.

The phrase "it has nothing to do with me" has become something of a fashion, and we may have the illusion that this severing of external ties is easy. But somewhere in their hearts the people who say this, and those who hear it, know that it is merely a sham, a feeble excuse. This is probably because the world has become smaller. As I said earlier, technology has made the world a single entity, and we have become conscious of it as such. But this single entity is split, and precisely because we cannot sever our relations with this divided entity, its splits are constantly invading our inner lives. This individual phenomenon is a microcosm of the modern world.

As an alternative to this attempt to work directly on a society split apart, we can consider the possibility of leaving society as it is and attempting to transcend it. This is the position of religion. Of course, there are many different religions, but the essential nature of any religion worthy of the name embodies in some form this impulse to transcend the secular world and the routine circumstances of daily life. In a certain sense, religion can be interpreted as a way of constructing a more inclusive *tatemae*; that is, one that goes beyond politics.

Consider the example of Jesus Christ, one of the great models of the religious life. Like the other Mediterranean countries in his age, the land of the Jews was under the control of the Roman Empire. The ruling class, while cooperating with Rome on the surface, contained a number of anti-Roman elements. There were also competing religious factions divided on the interpretation of Jewish doctrine. Into this situation came Christ, leading his own religious movement unaligned with any of the powerful political or religious groups. The great popular appeal of this new teaching earned him the antipathy and fear of the ruling factions.

One day, the Pharisees concocted a clever plot and asked Jesus if it was right or wrong to pay taxes to Rome. If he had answered that it is right, he would have provoked the anti-

Roman sentiments of the Jewish people. But if he had answered that it is wrong, he would have been labelled an anti-Roman provocateur and might well have been arrested on the spot by Roman soldiers. But Jesus saw through the trap, and the Pharisees had only set the stage for an embarrassing rebuke:

> "You hypocrites! Why are you trying to catch me out? Show me the money in which the tax is paid." They handed him a silver piece. Jesus asked, "Whose head is this, and whose inscription?" "Caesar's," they replied. He said to them, "Then pay Caesar what is due to Caesar, and pay God what is due to God." This answer took them by surprise, and they went away and left him alone.[3]

Jesus consistently refused to become embroiled in the splits in his society. Despite this, he was betrayed by one of his disciples and fell victim to the machinations of his opponents. Finally, he was charged with setting himself up as the king of the Jews and crucified by Roman officials. Just before his execution, however, he was asked by Pontius Pilate, "Are you the king of the Jews?" to which Jesus replied, "My kingdom does not belong to this world."[4] It is this position of earthly transcendence that has existed to this day as the essential spirit of Christianity.

However, to the extent that they exist in this secular world, no religion, and no religious believer, can cut all ties to this world. This is true not only of Christianity but of all religions. Moreover, when a religion grows strong enough to become a force in society, it is never left alone by the rulers of that society. The political establishment invariably attempts either to suppress or to use powerful religions. Religions themselves often exploit political forces in order to increase their own influence, sometimes even seizing secular political rule for themselves.

Recently, a number of religious leaders have begun taking the opposite approach, struggling against political authorities in the cause of social justice. These actions may deserve our admiration, and the thinking behind them should perhaps not be criticized. But we must also be aware that this kind of movement is often linked to a denial of the original spirit of religion, that of transcending the secular world. And it may even have the effect of splitting society further apart.

There is yet another approach that does not attempt to transcend societal divisions in the manner of religion, but instead seeks only to make us forget about them temporarily. This is the attempt to make a new world in a different dimension through creative activity. Of course, even in this case, reality cannot help but exert an influence, but to the extent that creation is possible, it is reality that is its fertilizer. Reality never obstructs creation, for the outstanding creative work itself forms a single unified world, without the kind of splits that exist in real societies.

In fact, creative activity is the special privilege of humanity, and it is impossible for us to measure how much charm it has lent to otherwise brutal and miserable lives. As I suggested above, however, when I quoted the famous opening passage of *Kusamakura*, not everyone who would leave this difficult world to live in a better one can become a poet. This is a built-in limit to the effectiveness of art. Moreover, even those who are capable of creating art may become physically or psychologically embroiled in the splits of society and find themselves no longer able to work.

We have been discussing up to now the various ways in which humanity has attempted to deal with divisions in society. But, of course, when these devices are no longer effective, the individual is directly exposed to societal splits. I would like to say a word here about situations in which people choose death as the final means of resisting splitting before things have reached this point. In fact, the number of people who chose this path in ancient times is by no means small, and this is as true of the West as of the East. Among them, we are especially moved by the stories of people who ended their own lives for pure motives. In Japan, one of the classic examples of such a person is Mama no Tegona, whose story is the subject of famous poems in the *Manyōshū* (*The Ten Thousand Leaves*), Japan's oldest anthology of poetry. A small Shintō shrine dedicated to her memory is still the object of religious worship.[5]

Tegona was renowned for her beauty and had a great number of suitors. Among them, two men in particular contended violently for her love. Confronted with their heated competition, however, Tegona felt increasingly uneasy about her marriage and finally ended her own life without saying which one of them she would choose. The two suitors, as if still vying with each other, both hurried to take their own lives.

What is important here is Tegona's reason for choosing death. It was not that she could not decide between the two men, or because she had chosen in her heart but could not tell them. Rather, she chose death because she was too modest to allow herself to be drawn inexorably into their contest. We can well imagine that it is for this pureness of motive that Tegona moved people's hearts so strongly, and that her story has been passed down to the Japanese through countless generations.

Having discussed the various means of preventing the occurrence of splits in human beings, I would now like to turn to an analysis of that splitting itself. In a seminal study based on the insights of phenomenology, the Dutch psychiatrist J. H. Van den Berg suggests that the phenomenon of the divided self was not addressed by specialists until the nineteenth century.[6] Although Van den Berg's analysis is mainly concerned with hysterical double personality, his argument is also useful in considering paranoid schizophrenia. Van den Berg also notes that hypnotic phenomena had been discovered at the end of the eighteenth century, and that the theme of double personality made its first appearance in literature at about the same time, as if psychiatry and literature were moving in the same direction simultaneously.

The most famous novel dealing with double personality, Robert Louis Stevenson's *The Strange Case of Dr. Jekyll and Mr. Hyde*, was published in 1886. Dostoyevsky's *The Double*, which depicts psychic phenomena closer to those of paranoid schizophrenia, was published in 1846. Why did the phenomenon of split personalities come into the spotlight during this period? In a word, it may be possible to say that all the various devices that were supposed to prevent the occurrence of splits in society had finally lost their effectiveness. As a result, *tatemae* and *honne* fell into sharp conflict and, no longer able to coexist, forced personalities to split.

Van den Berg explains this from the viewpoint of the sociocultural history of the West. The social and cultural changes of the period, which bore fruit in the French Revolution, eroded and then destroyed the traditional order. Class relations, which up to then had distinguished people from each other and linked them together, became vague, making human relations even more complex. The fact that people hated this complexity and sought to escape into simple human relationships accounts for the enormous vogue for hypnotism during this period in the West. Van den Berg suggests further that the publication in 1890 of William James's *Principles of Psychology*, in which James argued for the existence of many social selves, is proof that the multiple existences of human beings was finally generally recognized around this time.

It is interesting that Freud also entered the stage during this period, basing his research on clinical studies of hysteria. Freud's work would span half a century, and revolutionize our understanding of the human psyche, but in the beginning, Freud, like other scholars, accepted the double consciousness in hysteria at face value. From quite an early period, however, he opposed Pierre Janet's interpretation, which viewed the splitting of personality as the result of innate psychic weakness, and instead attempted to understand it by relating it to psychic conflicts. It was from this attempt that Freud developed his unique concept of the unconscious. For Freud, the unconscious was a kind of formula in which instinctual desires and impulses that are repulsed from consciousness continue to exist, and he interpreted the symptoms of hysteria and other mental illness as expressions of the unconscious desires and impulses that have been repulsed in this way in an altered form.[7]

What should be noted here is that, according to this interpretation, even when the personality appears at a glance to be split, the essential unity of the personality is in fact preserved, for repulsion occurs in order to maintain unity. Psychic conflicts arise precisely because the unity of the personality must be preserved. Stated in Van den Berg's terms, it is not impossible to say that Freud, with the concept of psychic conflicts, locked up the extremely dangerous phenomena of the divided self or the multiple existence of human beings inside the unconscious. Unconsciously, as it were, though not in the sense of the psychoanalytical concept, Freud used his own concept of the unconscious to make splits of personality into a matter of outward appearances. Heinz Hartmann, one of Freud's disciples, made a similar observation concerning the hypothetical question of why psychoanalysis had made its appearance in the West in the modern age.

> Apparently at certain points in history the ego can no longer cope with its environment, particularly not with that which it itself has created: the means and goals of life lose their orderly relation, and the ego then attempts to fulfill its organizing function by increasing its insight into the inner world.[8]

Thus, for Hartmann, psychoanalysis was an attempt to maintain psychic unity in a violently changing world by increasing insight into the inner world. However, the issue here is whether this attempt has in fact been successful. My own answer to this is yes and no. On the positive side, I think we can acknowledge that psychoanalysis has identified with considerable accuracy what it is that troubles us today, and that its prescription for dealing with that affliction is effective up to a certain point. The sociologist Phillip Rieff, for example, has written of psychoanalysis that it is "yet another method of learning how to endure the loneliness produced by culture." In a subsequent chapter, interestingly entitled "The Impoverishment of Western Culture," he suggests further that "a tolerance of ambiguities is the key to what Freud considered the most difficult of all personal accomplishments: a genuinely stable character in an unstable time."[9]

On closer examination, however, this demands a great deal of the individual. Only a very limited number of people could actually accomplish it. One reason for believing this is true is the fact that the distance between Freud's unconscious and today's reality is rapidly growing smaller. The unconscious is the unconscious precisely because reality stands in opposition to it. And, for this reason, if the unconscious and reality approach one another too closely, we lose the foothold that enables us to confront the unconscious as the unconscious. As Rieff suggests, we are still all right as long as we experience loneliness, but it is terrifying when, no longer able even to experience loneliness, and unable to distinguish between reality and the unconscious, we become submerged in our surroundings. In order to make this point even clearer, consider Freud's definition of the unconscious:

> The nucleus of the *Ucs*. [unconscious] consists of instinctual representatives which seek to discharge

their cathexis; that is to say, it consists of wishful impulses. These instinctual impulses are co-ordinate with one another, exist side by side without being influenced by one another, and are exempt from mutual contradiction. . . .

There is in this system no negation, no doubt, no degrees of certainty:. . . .

The processes of the system *Ucs*. are *timeless*; i.e. they are not ordered temporally, are not altered by the passage of time; they have no reference to time at all. . . .

The *Ucs*. processes pay just as little regard to *reality*. They are subject to the pleasure-principle; . . .

To sum up: *exemption from mutual contradiction, primary process* (mobility of cathexes), *timelessness,* and *replacement of external by psychical reality*— these are the characteristics which we may expect to find in processes belonging to the system *Ucs*.[10]

It is clear from this that Freud placed the unconscious at the opposite extreme from reality. But what are the most conspicuous phenomena in our contemporary reality? Is it not clear to anyone's eyes that they are precisely what Freud described as the characteristics of the unconscious? The satisfaction of desires, however extravagant, goes unchallenged. We avoid as much as possible anything that requires time or effort—the faster the better. So busy living from moment to moment, people almost never consider the meaning of human existence, which transcends the individual and continues from past to present to future. In a word, the trend is toward individualism. But despite this, or rather because of it, the individual becomes merely a cog in the machine, a cipher that can always be replaced. We lose sight of the human being—the irreplaceable individual. Of course, it would be impossible to argue that this tendency has made its first appearance in the modern world. It is at least true, however, that it has come to the forefront in our age.

In his *Hitler in Ourselves*, for example, Max Picard argues that it is just this kind of social ethos in the modern world that made the advent of Hitler possible: "Only in a world of total discontinuity could a nullity such as Hitler become Fuehrer, because only where everything is disjointed has comparison fallen into disuse."[11] As the title of the book suggests, Picard's bitter description of Hitler's genius is also a condemnation of modern society:

> Better than anybody else, Hitler knew that in this day and age time, permanence, and evolution within time no longer exist; he operated exclusively with the momentary in such a manner that the human being could not arrive at the distinction between good and evil.[12]

This is all too close to Freud's description of the unconscious. But, of course, it is difficult to believe that Picard was influenced by Freud in writing this. It seems much more likely that Freud, without realizing it, was influenced by the same modern conditions perceived by Picard when he defined his concept of the unconscious.

I believe that this drawing near of outer reality and the concept of the unconscious has operated subtly in the marked shift of emphasis that can be observed in recent psychoanalytic theory. While I do not mean to suggest that previous theories concerning instinctual drives and their repulsion have been discarded, it is certainly true that recent discussion has centered on the individual's object relations, and the splits that occur within them.

In Japanese, the word *taishō* (object) usually suggests

something non-human, but here, of course, it refers to human beings. The English word has its origins in Latin, and like the Japanese word *mono*, can be used to refer to both human beings and physical entities. Moreover, in psychoanalysis, the concept of splitting refers not to the real outer world, but to the individual's internal mental state. However, we cannot fail to acknowledge that the social and cultural conditions of modern society, which can only be described as split, are clearly reflected in the background of the fact that psychoanalysis has also come to deal directly with splits in personality.

Here I should explain briefly what is meant by splitting in recent developments in psychoanalysis. The term does not refer to gross phenomena of splits in personality that are considered to be clearly pathological, and are visible to anybody, such as hysterical double personality or schizophrenia. Rather, it refers to splitting that can be perceived by observing the human psyche more microscopically. Of course, the occurrence of this splitting can be perceived clearly in pathological mental conditions, but it can also occur in what appear at first glance to be normal conditions.

In order to explain this point, I would like to return to Sōseki's *Botchan*. What is characteristic of Botchan's human relations is that he immediately divides people into "good guys" and "bad guys." However, as we have seen in the case of Yamaarashi, even when someone has been labeled a "good guy," there is no telling when the label will change to the opposite extreme. And this has little to do with the people themselves, who become "good guys" or "bad guys" depending on what is convenient for Botchan. Botchan believes that he is always consistent, but viewed from the outside, it is ultimately he himself who changes "like the rolling of a cat's eyes."

To explain this in more concrete terms, the times when Botchan feels good because he has been allowed to *amaeru* by the other person—that is, when he has been indulged—and times when he feels bad because he has not been allowed to *amaeru* are not unified in a single self, and he blames his feelings on others. The fact that he gives all of his colleagues derogatory nicknames suggests that his relations with others are partial object relations based on a split ego, rather than mature relationships based on a recognition that others and he himself are independent personalities. And so it is not surprising that these relations do not last long. Earlier, I gave Botchan as an example of the person who is all *honne*, and it must be noted here that his personality is not unified by this insistence on *honne* but is instead split apart by it.[13]

As I pointed out above, the concept of splitting in psychoanalysis refers to the individual. But I must emphasize that what is characteristic of the modern age is the fact that this kind of splitting is shared by a great number of people—if not by most people. And as Max Picard suggests, what is important in the modern age is the fact that this condition is extremely convenient for anyone who would seize another's heart and mind, just as Botchan, no matter how much he hates Redshirt, is twisted around his little finger. Because his self is split apart, he does not recognize contradictions for what they are, and unable to distinguish between what is true and what is a lie, is easily taken in by Redshirt's propaganda.

We could call this "split-thinking," and it is precisely the same thing as Orwell's "doublethink" in *Nineteen Eighty-Four*.

> To know and not know, to be conscious of complete truthfulness while telling carefully constructed lies, to hold simultaneously to two opinions which cancelled out, knowing them to be contradictory and believing in both of them, to use logic against logic, to repudiate morality while laying claim to it, to believe that democracy was impossible and that the Party was the guardian of democracy, to forget whatever it

was necessary to forget, then to draw it back to memory again at the moment when it was needed, and then promptly to forget it again: and above all, to apply the same process to the process itself. That was the ultimate subtlety: consciously to induce unconsciousness, and then, once again, to become unconscious of the act of hypnosis you had just performed. Even to understand the word "doublethink" involved the use of doublethink.[14]

Orwell's doublethink occurs in the context of control by a totalitarian political system, and it is nothing less than uncanny that this kind of thinking appears to be pervasive in today's society, unrelated to any particular kind of political system. I find it extremely ominous that Orwell's pessimistic view of 1984 is so close to contemporary reality, and to the pervasive phenomenon of individuals split apart.

Notes

1. William James, *The Principles of Psychology* (New York: Dover Publications, 1950), 1:294.

2. G. H. Mead, *Mind, Self and Society* (Chicago: University of Chicago Press, 1934), 144.

3. Matthew 22:18–22. Biblical quotations are from *The New English Bible New Testament* (Middlesex, England: Penguin Books, Oxford University, and Cambridge University Press, 1964).

4. John 18:32–36.

5. Mama no Tegona (also Mama no Tekona or Mama no Otome) is one of the famous beauties of ancient times. The Shintō shrine dedicated to her is in the Mama district of Ichikawa City in present day Chiba prefecture. The *Manyōshū* is Japan's oldest extant royal anthology of poetry. It contains two poems on Tegona, by Yamabe Akahito and Takahashi no Mushimaro. [For the first volume of a complete translation in English, see Ian Levy, trans., *The Ten Thousand Leaves*, vol. 1 (Princeton: Princeton University Press; Tokyo: Tokyo University Press, 1981).—Trans.]

6. J. H. Van den Berg, *Divided Existence and Complex Society* (Pittsburg: Duquesne University Press, 1974).

7. The phrase "repulsed from consciousness" corresponds to what is usually called "repression." Here, I am following Bettleheim, who points out that the original German word, *Verdrängung*, does not mean "repression," but "repulsion." See Bruno Bettleheim, *Freud and Man's Soul* (New York: Vintage Books, 1982). See also Freud's own paper in English on the unconscious (published in 1912): "A Note on the Unconscious in Psycho-Analysis," in *The Standard Edition of the Complete Psychological Works of Sigmund Freud* (London: The Hogarth Press, 1971), 12:260–266. See also "Repression," (14:146–158), in which Freud states, "Repression is a preliminary state of condemnation (*Voruteilung*), something between flight and condemnation." (Personally, I feel that the word *Voruteilung* is closer to "censure.")

8. Heinz Hartmann, *Ego Psychology and the Problem of Adaptation* (New York: International Universities Press, 1961), 71.

9. Phillip Rieff, *The Triumph of the Therapeutic* (New York: Harper and Row, 1966), 32, 57.

10. "The Unconscious," *Standard Edition*, 14:186–187.

11. Max Picard, *Hitler in Our Selves*, Heinrich Hauser, trans. (Hinsdale, Illinois: Henry Regnery Company, 1947), 31.

12. Ibid., 51.

13. Admittedly, Botchan's nicknames for his colleagues are ingenious. Akashatsu (Redshirt) is a combination of the Chinese character for "red" and the *katakana* (*shatsu*) for "shirt," and this sobriquet refers not only to his red shirt itself, but also his Western affectations. Tanuki (raccoon dog) has connotations similar to those of "badger" or "fox" in English. Nodaiko (the word is derived from *Taikomochi* which means court jester) is a country bumpkin who plays the sycophant to Redshirt. Yamaarashi (Porcupine) is an apt label for his sometime friend, who is physically powerful and totally uncompromising.

14. George Orwell, *Nineteen Eighty-Four* (Middlesex: Penguin Books, 1984), 35.

PART THREE

THE SIGNIFICANCE
OF SECRETS

Chapter Seven

The Mind and Secrets

Now I would like to return to my starting point and take up the problem of *omote* and *ura* from a slightly different angle. First, by its very nature *kokoro* (the mind, the heart, subjectivity, intentionality) cannot be seen. Therefore, to say that people have an *omote* and an *ura*, and that *ura* is concealed behind *omote*, is essentially the same thing as to say that people have secrets (*himitsu*). The reader may well think that I have said very little by making this observation, but what I want to emphasize here is this: It is often said that *kokoro* is expressed in words and actions, but this does not mean that *kokoro* itself has been seen or heard. One person can read another's *kokoro* through his or her words and actions precisely because the one who listens and watches also has a *kokoro*. Therefore, *kokoro* itself remains hidden.

The existence of hypocrisy and deception, in which words and actions seem to express *kokoro* but in fact misrepresent it, is possible because this is true. Of course, if the person who is the object of hypocrisy or deception is astute enough, he or she may see through the pretense. Thus, the fact that *kokoro* is hidden is not what makes hypocrisy and deception evil. Rather, it is the fact that the person has pretended that there is something in his or her *kokoro* that is not there. It is usually no mistake, moreover, to take a suspicious view of any situation in which there is some ulterior motive for showing another person one's *kokoro*, even if there is no conscious intention to deceive. Surely one ought to say and do what one believes is right and appropriate. But even then one must beware of the quality of secrecy that is implicitly present in *kokoro*.

Here, I should perhaps say a word about the fact that I have used the word secrets, despite its often unfavorable connotations. The Japanese sometimes say that something "has the smell of secrecy." All too often this refers to something that somehow is not good—something people are afraid to put on public display, but the true nature of which we feel should ultimately be exposed. Of course, when we speak of the secrets of nature, or the secret of life, or the secret of personal charm, the connotation is by no means bad; nevertheless, even in these cases, it contains the implication that these secrets are a challenge to the human spirit, and the expectation that the veil of secrecy must eventually be removed.

These connotations are of relatively recent origin. They certainly did not exist in the distant past. *Himitsu*, the Japanese word for "secret," was originally a Buddhist term for dogma so profound that it could not easily be revealed to human beings. In its modern meaning, the word *shinpi* (mystery), which shares a Chinese character with *himitsu*,[1] also may suggest something dubious. But this word too originally referred to things unfathomable to human intellect; that is, "the secrets of the gods."

Thus, the tendency to think of secrets as something that should not exist, and ultimately as something that must not exist, is a phenomenon of the modern age. There is reason to believe that this tendency first appeared in the nineteenth century. Various facts point to this, but here I will allude to only one of them, the publication of Feuerbach's *The Essence of Christianity* in 1841.[2] A glance at the table of contents reveals a long list of titles containing the word "secret": The Secret of the Suffering God; The Secret of the Trinity; The Secret of Mysticism, or of Nature in God; The Secret of the Resurrection and of the Miraculous Conception. Looking at this array of titles, it is as if one were perusing a religious text. In fact, Feuerbach does cite a great number of religious and theological texts. But he does so expressly in order to wrest Christianity from "the false or theological essence of religion" and restore it to the realm of "the true anthropology," and he exerts all of his energies in this effort. He attempts to demonstrate that the doctrines of Christianity are not secrets transcending human intellect, but in every case extremely natural and human. If they are natural and human, then they are no longer secrets. This is Feuerbach's essential premise, and it is an early indication of modern humanity's extreme dislike of anything that transcends its own intellect. Indeed, people in the modern age believe that there must be nothing that transcends human intellect. We are driven—compelled—to make clear anything, everything, that is said to be "secret." I believe that it is from this that the modern spirit was born, a human spirit that tends to pay no attention to concealed *kokoro*.

In contrast to this modern spirit, all ancient teachings have in common the belief that the human heart (*kokoro*) is secret by its very nature, and that it must be kept secret. In *The Analects of Confucius*, for example, we find this: "Fine words and an insinuating countenance are seldom associated with virtue." Thus, Confucius (ca.551–ca.479 B.C.) argues that when the heart is employed in cleverness of speech or flattery, the true heart, the real *kokoro*, is often missing.

Jesus also taught the importance of secrets, and it is especially worth noting that he emphasized that God is hidden in a secret place.

"Be careful not to make a show of your religion

before men; if you do, no reward awaits you in your Father's house in heaven.

"Thus, when you do some act of charity, do not announce it with a flourish of trumpets, as the hypocrites do in synagogue and in the streets to win admiration from men. I tell you this: they have their reward already. No; when you do some act of charity, do not let your left hand know what your right is doing; your good deed must be secret, and your Father who sees what is done in secret will reward you.

"Again, when you pray, do not be like the hypocrites; they love to say their prayers standing up in synagogue and at the street-corners, for everyone to see them. I tell you this: they have their reward already. But when you pray, go into a room by yourself, shut the door, and pray to your Father who is there in the secret place; and your Father who sees what is secret will reward you."[3]

This emphasis on the importance of secrets is not limited to thinkers narrowly defined as religious or ethical. Among Zeami's most famous pronouncements on the Nō theater is the following:

Know the concealed flower. "What is concealed is the flower. What is not concealed cannot be the flower." To know this distinction is the flower, and among all flowers this flower is the most important. From the beginning, the respective houses in the various ways and arts have called all matters pertaining to their disciplines secrets, precisely because great work is done by making these matters secret.[4]

Some may find this suspicious, wondering why on earth it is so important to keep these things secret. Some may even be annoyed, feeling that it smacks of arcane mysticism—of privileging secrets for their own sake. As if to answer such doubts, Zeami continues with this:

> However, if what these houses call secrets are revealed, they are nothing of great note. But those who say that they are nothing of note do so precisely because they have not yet comprehended the matter of secrets.[5]

For Zeami, secrets did not exist because what they made secret was important. It was the fact of making something secret itself that was important.

In this connection, I wish to mention a Japanese custom, almost nonexistent today, that was once exemplary of a unique sensibility. In the traditional manner of gift-giving, the gift was first carefully wrapped in paper and then the package was wrapped again in a *furoshiki*.[6] Of course, the practice of wrapping gifts is by no means unique to Japan. What is unique are the greetings and other aspects of etiquette associated with the custom of wrapping (*tsutsumu*). The person presenting the gift would say, "Truly, this is only a symbol,"[7] or, "It is nothing special, but [please accept this],"[8] not making clear what was inside the package. The person receiving the gift would say, "For you to have exerted your heart (*kokoro*) so much on my behalf. . . ."[9] The receiver of a gift would never have asked what it was. Nor would they have opened the gift in front of the guest who had offered it.

I remember having been extremely irritated by this custom when I was a child. A guest would come bearing a gift, but I was not allowed to open it until after he or she left. It always seemed that the guest would never go home, and until they did, I couldn't see what was inside. When I went to the United

States shortly after the war, I was amazed to find that Americans opened presents right on the spot. This struck me as being eminently more rational.

Lately, however, I have begun to feel that there is a goodness in this custom that makes it difficult to discard. The gift of a present is a gift of the heart. The present, the thing itself, is merely a sign. Therefore, just as the heart is wrapped in flesh and cannot be seen from the outside, a gift must also be wrapped. And because this is true, to open a gift on the spot is unfeeling, an act without *kokoro*, and can even give the impression that one has not accepted it as a symbol of the other person's feelings, but simply with an eye to the thing itself. This beautiful custom of not opening gifts immediately has been almost completely lost, and I think it can be said that this is a result of the spirit of the age, an age which places no value on anything that is concealed.

Consider these statements by Friedrich Nietzsche, who dared to struggle against the spirit of his own age, but was himself destroyed in the struggle:

> Everything profound loves the mask. . . . Every profound spirit needs a mask: more, around every profound spirit a mask is continually growing.[10]

These words never fail to remind me of the old German saying: Still waters run deep. Apparently, Nietzsche reacted strongly against the loud clamor of his age, against a spirit that took Christian values for granted, indeed, as self-evident. Despairing of a modernism that had lost the sense of secrecy and fallen into decadence, he attempted over and over again to give his age a deeper spirituality to replace it, but in the end it was he who was defeated.

If it was Nietzsche who, as a philosopher, perceived that modern European society lacked real secrets, it was Freud, as a doctor, who first diagnosed the person suffering from an illness of the heart (*kokoro*) as one who had lost his or her own secrets. To be sure, Freud himself did not use the word in this sense. However, according to Freud's theory, mental illness occurs because what should be present to consciousness is not. Essentially, this is to say that the mentally ill have become unable to see what, by its very nature, must be present in their own hearts. In other words, they have lost sight of their own secrets.

Freud himself interpreted the word "secret" with all of its modern nuances and, like most outstanding scientists, he wanted to become one of the discoverers of nature's hidden secrets. In his biography of Freud, Ernest Jones describes a conversation they had on June 12, 1900:

> When I made the obvious remark about a tablet I did not know that years ago Freud had half-jokingly asked [Wilhelm] Fliess in a letter if he thought there would ever be a marble tablet on the spot bearing the inscription: "Here the secret of dreams was revealed to Dr. Sigm. Freud on July 24, 1885."[11]

So intent was he on discovering the secrets of the human psyche, and so convinced that he had discovered in dreams the clue to these secrets, that Freud apparently failed to perceive that secrets are indispensable to that psyche. And to the extent that this is exactly what his own theory of mental illness suggests, it is indeed ironic.

Next, I would like to look at various aspects of mental illness from the viewpoint of secrets. People who generally are called neurotics tend to seek various "causes" for what is troubling them, to blame their problem on something outside themselves. In fact, however, we can describe their condition by saying that without even realizing that they have secrets, they have more secrets than they can handle. In contrast, there are others who appear to be saying that they have no secrets at all. They have no resources available to them anymore. They are in trouble, and that's that. It can't be helped. Still others have fallen into a condition of panic, as if they were being deprived of their secrets. They feel exposed and defenseless. In this way, we can understand the various aspects of mental illness by relating them to the fact that these people are unable to have secrets. In order to help them, it is necessary to begin from the point at which we can make them become self-conscious of this fact.

The therapist, rather than trying to discover the secret of the illness, must first encourage the mentally ill person to wonder about his or her own condition. Every case is different, but ultimately this is a matter of guiding them to a realization of the fact that their problems are related to the nature of the secrets in their minds, which they had not been aware of before. Thus, we can say that they are liberated from the sickness in their hearts only when they can feel secure and can have their own secrets.

To sum up, the ideal condition of the mind—the condition from which mental health derives—is one in which we can feel comfortable with having secrets. Lest I be misunderstood, I should point out that this has nothing to do with arcanism or mysticism. To be comfortable with our secrets does not mean to shut them up within ourselves. We communicate what is necessary to others. If we are mentally healthy, we realize that we have secrets, that there are things inside us that we could not communicate to others even if we wanted to. Furthermore, the healthy person does not feel that having secrets is painful. We feel a profound sense of wonder at their presence, but we accept them as part of the gift of being human.

To describe this condition of mental health only in these terms would be to make it seem all too abstract. It can be explained in more tangible terms. In my opinion, the best way to describe it is as a condition in which one has something to spare. I think anyone can understand this. But it is not so easy to explain why "having something to spare" (*yutori ga aru*) corresponds to the condition of having secrets.

First, having something to spare can apply not only to the mind but also to things. In Japan, for instance, and especially in Tokyo, we often yearn for a "space in which there is some extra room." People everywhere wish for "a little spare money." However, if we examine these expressions more closely, it becomes clear that we are not really talking about space or money themselves, but how they can be used. Regardless of how much space or money we may have, if conditions are such that it is absolutely impossible to use them, then we really have nothing to spare. The same is true if the way we can use them is closely prescribed. To have something to spare is to be able to use it if we want to, and not to have restrictions on how we do so. To have something to spare is to have set aside space or money that can be used if some unforeseen situation arises.

The same thing can be said for time. To have spare time does not mean that one is usually not busy. There are people who seem to have more time than they know what to do with, but I would not say that these people have time to spare. As in the case of space or money, to have time to spare is to be able to make time for something if you want to. This is related to the condition of the mind. In a word, what I am referring to here is the use of the useless, and it is this that reveals the degree of internal freedom of the mind. For example, when we are working on something, our minds are turned to whatever we are doing, but if we have something—whether time or money—to spare, we never become slaves to our work. If necessary, we can always pull our attention away from it. Call this the spirit of play. Of course there is nothing to spare when giving oneself up completely to play either. In order for us really to have something to spare, we must maintain a delicate balance between play and seriousness, and between freedom and restraint.

The problem is how to achieve this balance—how to reach this condition of having something to spare. It is clear that it is a highly desirable condition, if not the ideal state of the mind. But it is not so clear how we can achieve it. At a conference in Salzburg sponsored by the World Federation for Mental Health in 1979, I was asked to explain the concept of *yutori* in English, and it was on this point that I had the most difficulty. I was able to explain that it was related to the ability to distinguish what is most important, and that it was profoundly related to the problem of values, but I had to end my part of the discussion there, begging off with the excuse that if I went any further I would be in danger of losing my own *yutori*. At the time, it was only an excuse, made in desperation, but later I realized that without being aware of it I had said something extremely important. That is, in order to have *yutori* it is necessary to keep secret what it is that is most important to oneself. Otherwise, one's freedom is lost, and one is no longer able to create something to spare when it is needed. There are no blank spaces or free time to fill, and one can no longer produce them.

The old Japanese expression "a place in the heart to depend on" (*kokoro ni tanomu tokoro*) describes the same spiritual condition implied by *yutori*. In 1983, I spoke again on the subject of *yutori* at the International Conference on Values. I cited the same passage from Zeami that I quoted above: "What is not concealed cannot be the flower." And I concluded my speech by saying that *yutori* is the flower of living, and that it cannot bloom without secret values.

Notes

1. *Himitsu* 秘密. *Shinpi* 神秘.

2. For the standard English translation of this book, see Ludwig Feuerbach, *The Essence of Christianity*, George Eliot, trans. (New York: Harper & Row, Publishers, 1957). However, Eliot appears to have misunderstood the German *Geheimnis*, which is usually translated "secret."

3. Matthew 6:2–6.

4. Zeami Motokiyo, *Fūshi Kaden* [Teachings on Style and the Flower], in *Zeami Geijutsuron Shū* [Collection of Zeami's Treatises on Performance Arts], *Shinchō Nihon Koten Shūsei* [Shinchō Compendium of the Japanese Classics], 4 (Tokyo: Shinchōsha, 1983), 92. [For a complete translation in English of Zeami's treatises, see J. Thomas Rimer and Yamazaki Masakazu, trans., *On the Art of the Nō Drama: The Major Treatises of Zeami* (Princeton: Princeton University Press, 1984). Zeami (1363–1443) established the Nō drama as the preeminent performance art of Japan. For him, the concept of "the flower" (*hana*) was even more important than that of *yūgen*. It was the perfect metaphor for the ineffable charm of a performance by a great actor.—Trans.]

5. Ibid.

6. [A *furoshiki* (bath cloth) is a rather large piece of square fabric, usually silk. As its name suggests, it was originally used to carry toilet items and a change of clothes when one went to the public bath. From very early on, however, its uses as a carry-all were almost universal. It is still used frequently for wrapping wedding presents and gifts for other formal occasions.—Trans.]

7. これはほんとにおしるしです。

8. つまらぬものですが。

9. そんなにお心遣いして頂いて。

10. Friedrich Nietzsche, *Beyond Good and Evil*, R. J. Hollingdale, trans. (Middlesex, England: Penguin Books, Ltd., 1984), 51.

11. Ernest Jones, *The Life and Work of Sigmund Freud* (New York: Basic Books, 1953), 1:354.

Chapter Eight

Secrets and Charm

In the previous chapter, I stated that the ideal state of the heart (*kokoro*) is one in which the individual is able to keep secrets and I think this is related to what we often call the charm of personality. I say this because it appears that the secret of an attractive personality is ultimately related to whether or not there is something secret in that personality. Is it not true, in fact, that nothing attracts people more than a secret? In this chapter, I would like to explain this point by considering a number of well-known personalities in real life and literature.

There are many people who possess attractive personalities, but let us begin here with the poet-priest Ryōkan (1758–1831), whose charm appeals to the hearts of Japanese as much today as during his own lifetime.[1] As is suggested by the fact that he spent most of his life as a Zen recluse, the most striking thing about Ryōkan was that he valued his own inner life above everything else. It is clear in his poetry that he truly enjoyed living in seclusion.

> It is not that
> I would shun completely
> Worldly affairs,
> But solitary pleasure
> I find much better.[2]

There are many anecdotes depicting Ryōkan's unique personality. One of the most interesting for our discussion is about an occasion when he was playing hide-and-seek with some children. Unable to find him, the children gave up and went home, but Ryōkan remained in his hiding place until nightfall. Other than the mental states he occasionally expressed in his poetry, Ryōkan never spoke about himself, and his biographers tell us that he never gave sermons or lectures on the sutras. The one exception to this is his *Kaigo* (Prohibitions), a collection of aphorisms concerning daily conversation, but the aphorisms themselves only serve as further proof of how highly he valued what he had secreted in his own heart. They reveal Ryōkan's awareness of the fact that words can never express the heart completely, and this knowledge made him exceedingly discrete with words. Here are some examples from the *Kaigo*:

An excess of words

Glibness

Stories no one asked for

Gratuitous advice

Bragging of one's exploits

Speaking before another person has finished

Teaching others something one does not really understand oneself

Speaking indecently

Speaking pretentiously

Speaking of this matter before one has finished that matter

Intruding into people's conversations

Saying things in a kindly seeming manner

Speech reeking of the scholar

Speech reeking of elegance

Speech reeking of Zen enlightenment
Speech reeking of the tea master
In all things, words should be spoken with sincerity.[3]

Ryōkan apparently made a deep impression on the people who came into contact with him. In *Ryōkan Zenji Kiwa* (Strange Stories of the Zen Priest Ryōkan), Kera Yoshishige (1810–1859) describes him as follows:

> The master was always silent, his movements tranquil, as if there were something more. . . . To spend a single night talking with the master was to feel a pureness of the heart. The master never preached the sutras, Japanese or foreign; nor did he encourage good deeds. Sometimes he would be burning a fire by the kitchen; sometimes he would be doing *zazen* meditation in the main chapel. His words did not extend to poetry, and they did not reach to moral principles, but were quiet, nonchalant, completely beyond description.[4]

Ryōkan may truly be said to have been a person who possessed *yutori*, in the sense explained earlier. What is most important to note in this description is that there is not the slightest hint that Ryōkan was difficult to approach. On the contrary, he aroused feelings of fondness in all those who came into contact with him. In short, Ryōkan possessed what I believe to be the two essential qualities of the human being who has charm: an interior life that is indiscernible from the outside, and the ability to arouse feelings of intimacy in others. More will be said about these qualities below, but first I would like to give a second example of a person who possessed this kind of charm.

That person is none other than Jesus Christ. It would perhaps be more appropriate to simply call him Jesus. I say this because Christ is a religious title, and while it is common today to use it as part of his name, Jesus's secret was precisely the fact that he was Christ. His life is veiled in secrecy from the moment of his birth, although there is no evidence that this attracted people's attention during his lifetime. He spent the first thirty years of his life as an ordinary, anonymous person. He seems quite literally to have appeared from nowhere one day, an unknown Jewish rabbi. But his powerful teachings and miraculous acts of healing immediately attracted attention.

Christ himself always attempted to avoid his own reputation. Especially when he performed miraculous acts of healing he would sternly admonish the person who had been healed not to speak of it to others. Whenever the mob attempted to make him the figurehead for some political act, he would quietly slip away. Moreover, he never made a point of announcing to people that he was Christ. One day, he gathered his disciples in an isolated spot and asked them what the people were calling him. After listening to their answers, he asked them the same question: What do you call me? When one of his disciples answered, "You are Christ," he sternly warned them never to repeat this to anyone, and then began to tell them about his imminent death and resurrection. Soon after this, he fell into the hands of those who viewed him as an enemy and died on the cross, ending a public career that had lasted only two or three years. On the third day after the crucifixion, the gospels report that he was miraculously resurrected from the grave, but even this was an experience shared only by his disciples and a few other intimates.

Thus, Jesus's life, and its meaning, were shrouded in secrecy, and the essence of that secret has not been penetrated even today. The outlines of the secret are known. In that sense, it is an open secret. But the quality of secrecy remains just as before. What is known is only that certain things about Jesus were kept secret, but there is nothing else to prove that the contents of these secrets were facts. On the other hand, it has also been impossible to deny Jesus's secrets by proving that the true facts were otherwise. And yet, for two thousand years, people have been attracted to these secrets and have believed in their universal significance. Even today, millions of Christians scattered all over the globe share this belief.

While their charm is universal, both Ryōkan and Jesus were religious figures, and their cases may seem rather special. I would now like to turn to a more general example, which is to be found in Natsume Sōseki's *Kokoro*.[5] Sōseki himself was quite pleased with this work and even went so far as to write an advertising blurb for the first Iwanami edition:

> To those who desire to grasp their own hearts (*kokoro*), I recommend this work, which has succeeded in grasping the hearts (*kokoro*) of human beings.[6]

I agree with this assessment, and I have had many occasions to discuss the rich insights in this novel from a wide range of perspectives.[7] This time, I would like to focus on how it illustrates the relationship between secrets and charm.

Kokoro begins with the first encounter between the first-person narrator, a university student, and the older man he will come to call Sensei.[8] This meeting occurs quite by accident at a resort in Kamakura, where the student is enjoying his summer vacation. After they return to Tokyo, the student becomes a frequent visitor to Sensei's home. The relationship between "I" and Sensei is the axis on which the novel turns, but one is led to ask why the young man is attracted to Sensei in the first place. "I" answers this himself, by saying that he had immediately felt a sense of *déja vù* on their first encounter, a sense of intimacy that made him feel as if he had met this man before. More important for our present discussion is that he continues this explanation with the following observation of Sensei:

> From the beginning, I had felt that there was
> something strange about Sensei that made it difficult
> to approach him. But, even so, somewhere at work
> was the strong feeling that I could not help but ap-
> proach him.[9]

The relationship between the young man and his father is the
direct opposite. When he returns home to the country from
Tokyo, he finds his father boring and countrified, and he
realizes why: "I knew almost everything there was to know
about my father."[10]

One day, the young man tells Sensei that his father is ill, and
then listens in surprise as Sensei, unusually excited, warns him
to settle the matter of his inheritance as quickly as possible.
When he asks why, Sensei tersely explains that he had been
cheated out of his own inheritance by his uncle and that this is
the cause of his misanthropy. Not satisfied with this, "I" presses
Sensei to tell him more about his past on another occasion. At
first, Sensei refuses, but when the younger man persists, he
becomes visibly shaken and finally promises to reveal his past
to "I." He has come this far not trusting anyone, but now he
wants to believe in at least one other human being before he
dies. If the young man is really sincere, he will tell him
everything about himself. However, this promise also contains
a warning and a condition.

> I will tell you. I will tell you everything about my
> past, leaving nothing out. . . . But my past may not
> be as profitable to you as you think. It might be better
> not to hear about it. Moreover—moreover, I will not
> tell you immediately. Accept that, for I will not tell
> you unless the right occasion presents itself.[11]

Sensei's attitude may seem to be terribly pompous, but subsequent developments make it clear that this is by no means true. Not long after this confrontation, Sensei commits suicide, but before taking his own life, he fulfills his promise by writing down the secret of his past in a long letter and sending it to "I." It is a secret he has never before revealed to anyone, not even his own wife. The letter is an autobiography in the form of a last will and testament. It is the story of a truly tragic life. The reader, who is not involved in the story, and especially a psychiatrist, would wonder immediately if it had not been written by someone mentally ill. Strangely enough, however, "I" does not interpret it in this way at all. Far from losing his feeling of respect for Sensei after reading it, "I's" story, the novel itself, becomes an expression of the younger man's profound understanding, and of his love for Sensei.

> A person who could love human beings, a person indeed who could not help loving human beings, but a person who even so could not open his arms to embrace those who attempted to enter his heart—that was Sensei.[12]

In short, the secret of Sensei's past is the rupture of a human relationship. It is also this that finally drove him to commit suicide. But in the final moment he was able to share his secret with "I." It is not that his secret was found out, but rather that it was accepted by the younger man as a secret. At the beginning of his letter, Sensei writes, "Now, I myself am about to tear open my own heart and spray your face with its blood. If, when my pulse stops beating, a new life dwells in your breast, I will be satisfied."[13] "I" is able to respond with love to this expression of Sensei's love for him.

In the case of "I" and Sensei, the revealing of Sensei's secret did not destroy their relationship. In real life, however, when one person's secret becomes known to the other person in a relationship, the relationship is often dealt a decisive blow. It is in this situation that feelings of betrayal arise. These feelings can be considered the root cause of ruptures in relationships between men and women, and of the cooling of relations that occurs between parents and children, or even between friends.

There is little need to explain how the disclosure of secrets can effect relationships between men and women, but it is somewhat more complex in the case of parents and children. When a child is small, the parent is an awesome, even frightening, presence. At the same time, the child is an object of hope for the parent. In short, both the parent and the child are still unknown to each other. However, far from disturbing their relationship, this fact has the opposite effect of binding them even more closely together. As proof of this, we need only consider the fact that parent and child tend to drift apart as the child grows up and they are both able to see each other as they really are.

The relationship between "I" and his father in *Kokoro* is a good example. "I" tells us, "I knew almost everything there was to know about my father. If I were to be separated from Father, only regret for the lost affection between parent and child would remain in my heart."[14] But his father is also aware of the coolness that has developed in their relationship: "Educating children is both good and bad. You help them so they can pursue their studies, and then they never come home again. It's as if you educate children just to estrange them from their parents."[15] This section of *Kokoro*, which is entitled "My Parents and I," is the story of "I's" alienation from his father, and its theme is the fact that the more two people in a relationship come to know about each other, the more their mutual secrets are disclosed, and the more the relationship becomes something cold and insipid.

It is apparently for this reason that people will go to extreme lengths to create secrets when they can no longer sense an air of secrecy in their surroundings. Without secrets, life is dull. Tanizaki Junichirō (1886–1965) develops this theme in his short story *Himitsu* (The Secret).[16] At the beginning of the story, the hero, bored with his life as a self-indulgent playboy, has slipped away from the company of his wealthy friends and is living incognito at a temple in the Asakusa district of Tokyo. He explains why he has chosen this particular method of stimulating his jaded sensibilities in the following way:

> I had deliberately hidden myself in an obscure place in the lower city, where no one would notice me, out of the desire to experience once more feelings like those I had felt playing hide-and-seek in my childhood.[17]

The hero's desire to reexperience the feelings of a child playing hide-and-seek is highly significant, for this kind of play is the first chance for children to become aware of secrets as secrets. He himself puts this very succinctly:

> I had tasted the thrilling interest of secrets since childhood. Games like hide-and-seek, treasure hunting, and blind man's buff—especially when they were played on a dark night, or in a gloomy storage shed, or before imposing double doors—surely the main *cause* of the interest I felt in those moments was the uncanny mood of "secrecy" in which they were veiled.[18]

After settling into his room at the temple, he experiments with various disguises, and finally hits upon the idea of disguising himself as a woman. He slips away from the temple every night to roam through the streets in this guise, experiencing an ineffable excitement at his success in transforming himself into a woman. His nocturnal wanderings allow him to peer into a new, secret world even while he himself remains concealed.

One night, he is sitting in a movie theater when he realizes that the person next to him is a woman with whom he had had a fleeting affair. She too has seen through his disguise and recognizes him as an old lover. They agree to resume their affair, but the woman insists on some rather peculiar arrangements. They are not to reveal to each other their present circumstances, or even where they live. Whenever they are to meet, she will send a rickshaw for him, and he will be blindfolded before being taken to her home. The rickshaw will take a complicated route, making seemingly endless turns so that he cannot make out even the direction in which it is travelling.

Night after night, he meets the woman in this fashion, reveling in the secrecy of these mysterious rendezvous. But then he begins to feel the urge to find out her secret, to search out the location of her home and discover who she really is. He sets off one day to retrace the route taken by the rickshaw each time they had met, hoping that his instincts will guide him to the right place. After nearly a full day of searching, he finally finds himself standing before what seems to be the right house. Looking up, his eyes meet those of the woman, who happens to be leaning over the second-floor railing watching the passersby. Instantly, her face is clouded with disappointment, and at the same moment his attraction to her fades. He turns away to leave without even exchanging greetings with her, and their relationship is over. A few days later, he leaves his hiding place to return to life in high society. The artificial secrecy of the world he has constructed, once destroyed, has lost its magical power.

With *Kokoro* and *Himitsu* in mind, I would like to return to our discussion of the essential qualities of the charming personality: possession of an inner life that is indiscernible from the outside, and the ability to arouse feelings of intimacy in others. The German word for secret, *Geheimnis*, is very interesting for such a discussion, for it contains the word *Heim*, which means "home." *Heimlich*, which is now always used as an adjective meaning "secret" or "hidden," also contains *Heim*. According to a German dictionary, this is no accident. Originally, *heimlich* meant simply "belonging to the home," or, by extension, "intimate." The modern meaning of "secret" appeared in the twelfth century and gradually became predominant.[19] Thus, at least in German, the words "secret" and "intimate" are linked by "home." This is no doubt due to the fact that the home is a special place. For those who belong to it, the home is a place for relaxation and mutual intimacy, but for anyone outside, it is a place of secrets. The evolution in the meaning of the German word *heimlich* is an excellent model of the structure of charm. The home is an entity that is indiscernible from the outside, but despite that fact, or rather because of it, it arouses feelings of desire to partake of its intimacy.

The antonym of *heimlich* is *unheimlich*, which is often translated as "weird," or "frightening," but it can also mean "uncanny." In any case, the word refers to the opposite of that which is charming. Freud himself appears to have been extremely interested in the relationship between these two words, and a long paper on "the uncanny" is well-known among his literary essays.[20]

Even without citing Freud's work, the very different endings of *Kokoro* and *Himitsu* can be considered from the perspective offered by the fact that *unheimlich* means the opposite of charming. When the hero of *Himitsu* discovered the woman's house and realized that she was in fact quite ordinary, what he felt was not simply disillusionment. Of course, he was disillusioned. The secret world that he had constructed in his fantasies had been destroyed at a single stroke. But he was also made to confront the uncanniness of the reality all around him, to realize that life itself is *unheimlich*.

In Sōseki's *Kokoro*, it would have been natural for the young man to feel disillusioned, and even frightened, when he learns from Sensei's letter that his revered mentor had had something so shameful in his past that he had hidden it until his suicide, but "I" experiences neither of these emotions. We have asked why, and I suggested earlier that it is because the younger man is able to accept Sensei's secret as a secret. Now I can suggest that this acceptance is also the reason he does not feel *unheimlich* at the knowledge of Sensei's secret. What makes this possible is nothing other than love, in this case, the love that has developed between "I" and Sensei. It appears that a special relationship exists between secrets and love, and that is the subject of my next chapter.

Notes

1. Ryōkan was the most important Japanese poet of his age, having produced some fourteen hundred poems in Japanese and four hundred in Chinese. [For a biographical sketch and a selection of his poetry in translation, see Nobuyuki Yuasa, *The Zen Poems of Ryōkan* (Princeton: Princeton University Press, 1981).—Trans.]

2. See Yoshino Hideo, *Ryōkan Shū* [Ryōkan's Japanese Poems], *Koten Nihon Bungaku Zenshū* [Compendium of Classical Japanese Literature] (Tokyo: Chikuma Shobō, 1966), 21, poem 1040.

3. Cited in Karaki Junzō, *Ryōkan* (Tokyo: Chikuma Shobō, 1971).

4. Ibid., 52–53. [*Ryōkan Zenshi Kiwa* was published c. 1845.—Trans.]

5. Natsume Sōseki, *Kokoro*, *Sōseki Zenshū* [The Complete Works of Natsume Sōseki] (Tokyo: Iwanami Shoten, 1966), 6:3–288. [For a complete English translation, see Sōseki Natsume, *Kokoro*, Edwin McClellan, trans. (Chicago: Henry Regnery, 1957; London: Peter Owen, 1967; Tokyo: Tuttle, 1969). Kokoro was first published in 1914.—Trans.]

6. *Soseki Zenshū*, 11:517.

7. See, for example, Doi Takeo, *The Psychological World of Natsume Sōseki*, William J. Tyler, trans. (Cambridge: Harvard University Press, 1976), 105–126.

8. *Sensei* is a polite form of address indicating respect for another person's age or experience. It is used by students when addressing or referring to their teachers. As in *Kokoro*, its meaning is often closer to that of the English word mentor, or the French *maître*, suggesting a closer relationship than such titles as Professor or Doctor.

9. *Kokoro*, 18.

10. Ibid., 122.

11. Ibid., 86.

12. Ibid., 18.

13. Ibid., 154.

14. Ibid., 122–123.

15. Ibid., 118.

16. Tanizaki Junichirō, *Himitsu* [The Secret], in *Tanizaki Junichirō Zenshū* [The Complete Works of Tanizaki Junichirō] (Tokyo, Chūō Kōron-sha, 1966), 1:247–271.

17. *Himitsu*, 252.

18. Ibid.

19. Gerhard Wahrig, *Deutsches Wörterbuch* (Mosaik Verlag, 1980), 1744.

20. Sigmund Freud, "The Uncanny," *Standard Edition*, 17:219–252.

Chapter Nine

Secrets and Love

It is difficult even to imagine how many books have been written on the subject of love, but judging from the ones I have seen, surprisingly few of them have considered the subject from the viewpoint of love and secrets. When I glanced through the books on love in my own library, I could not find the word secrets anywhere in the tables of contents, or even in their indexes. Perhaps a more careful examination would have yielded a few paragraphs on what I want to consider in this chapter, but it seemed unlikely that I would find an extended discussion.

The one exception was a slim volume I had stumbled across at a bookstore, *Das Geheimnis der Liebe* (The Secret of Love), by the German theologian Hans Asmussen.[1] It turns out that this book is not very well known. It has not been translated into Japanese or English. Aside from the fact that he wrote the book, I know nothing about Asmussen or his reputation among German intellectuals. But when I read this book, I found myself responding to it wholeheartedly and thought to myself that Asmussen was saying exactly the same thing I want to discuss here. I will introduce his main conclusions below, but before doing so I would like to consider the relationship between secrets and love in terms of the examples given in the previous chapter.

In Sōseki's *Kokoro*, Sensei is a person who has lived his entire adult life under the crushing weight of his own secret, and had it not been for the appearance of "I," he would have had to carry that secret alone to his grave. But just before he commits suicide, he is able to reveal his secret to the young man who has idolized him. His intention in doing so is not merely to unburden himself by revealing his secret to another, but also to help the young man. He hopes that by sharing his past with "I" he will have given the younger man a source of guidance for living his own life. In this way, the long letter Sensei sends to "I," his last will and testament, is both a confession of his secret and a confession of his love for "I." His love for the young man is the source of the intensely emotional statement I quoted in the previous chapter: "If, when my pulse stops beating, a new life can dwell in your breast, I will be satisfied."[2] But why, we ask ourselves, does he confess his love in this dramatic manner? And why is he able to do so only at this moment, just before his own death? To be sure, we have been given ample suggestion that Sensei has never found the young man's devotion displeasing. Earlier in the story, he even asks "I" why he bothers to visit a person like himself so often. But it is not until he has decided to commit suicide that he is able to express his feelings directly to "I."

Sensei's reluctance to speak directly of his love can be explained by the fact that love, as we all know, is a very private emotion. It is not that easy for anyone to speak of feelings of love. In other words, love, by its very nature, is a secret of the heart, and it can only reveal itself as the confession of a secret. This is suggested by the fact that we use the same word, "confession," in speaking of both secrets and love. Of course, the fact that Sensei's secret is a failed human relationship—the fact that his whole life has been torn apart by love—may also be a factor in his reluctance to express his love for "I."

Sensei's secret is revealed in his letter to "I." He had lost his parents at an early age, and his uncle had become his guardian. At first things went well, but Sensei refused to marry his uncle's daughter, and their relationship became strained. Finally, he quarreled with his uncle over his father's estate and left, feeling cheated. Sensei had always been introverted, and after this experience he found himself unable to confide in anyone except his friend K. But he and K fell in love with the same woman. Sensei tricked K and proposed first, never suspecting that his friend would commit suicide after learning of his betrayal. Sensei married the woman without revealing the circumstances of K's death, and he had lived with this secret ever since, unable to confess it even to his wife.

But then "I" appears, a young man who idolizes him and wants to make him his mentor. His lonely life shut away from the world is suddenly disrupted. Sensei must have been astonished. At first, he states quite clearly that he is not the kind of person who could fulfill "I's" expectations. But even as he says this, he wants to trust the younger man, to find at least one person before he dies to whom he can tell the story of his past. Gradually he begins to feel love for "I" and his thinking changes. He is willing to reveal the secret of his past to "I" if it will help him—even more, he wants desperately to believe that it will help him. And the right time for him to carry out this plan finally presents itself when he is on the verge of taking his own life.

Thus, one of the many insights offered by Sōseki's *Kokoro* is the truth that love is fundamentally a secret of the heart, and that the confession of a secret is the same in essence as a confession of love. But this story takes place in a work of fiction, and it may strike the reader as an extremely special case. The story I want to return to next, the story of Jesus Christ, is from real life, but it too is a special story. In this case, however, I believe that what is special about the story suggests principles that are universal.

Even non-Christians know that Jesus preached a religion of love. One of the most famous of his teachings is from the Sermon on the Mount: "Do not set yourself against the man who wrongs you. If someone slaps you on the right cheek, turn and offer him your left."[3] On the night of his death, Jesus tells his disciples, "There is no greater love than this, that a man should lay down his life for his friends."[4] Of course, Jesus left much more to humanity than impressive aphorisms concerning love. Christians believe that his existence itself—his life and his death—are an incarnation of God's love.

It is interesting, however, that while love was the most important theme of his career, Jesus himself said very little about personal love. Of course, it cannot be true that Jesus did not have feelings of personal love, or that he did feel personal love but deliberately concealed it. Jesus loved people from his heart, and his disciples and many other people must have known his love directly. But Jesus rarely said, "I love you," and he was by no means always surrounded by an atmosphere of love. He attracted a huge following, but even while people were drawn to him, they viewed him with an awe that verged on fear, and some reacted strongly against the power of his teachings.

Two or three days before his death on the cross, Jesus was visited by a woman who loved him. What took place during this visit was a scene full of dark foreboding, for she anointed his head with an expensive perfumed oil. Jesus himself accepted this act as a preparation for his own burial, but the disciples failed to perceive the woman's insight and berated her for wasting the precious perfume. Even this close to the time of his death, Jesus's love had not succeeded in melting the hearts of his disciples. And it was on this same night that Judas offered to betray him to his enemies, as if reacting against the woman's act of love.

On the following night, Jesus gathered his disciples for their last supper together. He warned them of his impending death and revealed to them that his death was for their salvation. Jesus's farewell discourses during the Last Supper were in fact his first confession of love to his disciples. According to the Book of John, Jesus spoke most intimately to his disciples of his feelings for them after sending Judas away to meet his enemies. There is something extremely human in this act.

The story of Jesus has the same pattern as that of Sensei in Sōseki's *Kokoro*. Both men confess their love for the first time when they are already confronting death. Unlike Sensei, however, Jesus did not have another great secret to confess. His greatest secret was precisely that his death was the ultimate proof of his love. Seen in this light, I think it is possible to understand why he kept his real mission secret during his public career as a rabbi. And the fact that this man, whose mission itself was love, kept his love secret until the final moment is a clear indication of the general principle that love is one of the profoundest secrets of the heart.

In fact, the same principle can be seen in the most mundane love between men and women. For either a man or a woman, it is a shocking experience when someone begins to feel love toward another person. Before trying to express this love to the other person, he or she will first attempt to hide it. That is, the person in love first becomes isolated. Only after making sure that the other person will keep the secret of love will he or she confess love. In fact, as long as they are unsure of this, he or she may even make a pretense of not loving to disguise a feeling of deeper, truer love.

Romantic love has been the subject of so many literary works that one wonders if literature would exist without it. I think this is proof of how the secret of love takes control of people's hearts and refuses to let go. But to speak of the secret of love as a general concept is to say little of how this happens in reality. Also, how love, in the beginning a secret, is finally communicated to the loved one varies widely from case to case.

But it is precisely this that makes love so interesting and that has made it the wellspring for a virtually infinite number of literary texts. Here, let us consider how the secret of love is finally shared in one of the most famous love stories of all time, *Romeo and Juliet*.

Romeo, scion of the Montague family, falls in with a scheme devised by Mercutio and Benvolio to secretly attend a banquet at the house of the Capulet's, with whom his own family has an ancient quarrel. Wearing masks and mingling with the other guests, who are also masked, they succeed in gaining admission. Romeo sees Juliet and falls in love, unaware that she is Capulet's daughter, and she falls in love with him at first sight, also unaware that he is the son of her father's enemy. Once they know each other's identities, they are placed in the worst possible situation for lovers. But Shakespeare, with his inimitable finesse, allows them to leap over this obstacle with a single bound. As he and his friends are returning home from the party, Romeo slips away into the darkness and steals into the Capulet's orchard. Of course, he hopes to catch a glimpse of Juliet, or at least be near her, but he also wants to be alone, away from his friends, so that he can think about her. He never even dreams that they will share confessions of love on this night. But suddenly she appears on the balcony. Unaware that he is actually present, she pretends to herself that she is calling out to him: "O Romeo, Romeo! wherefore art thou Romeo? / Deny thy father and refuse thy name; / Or, if thou wilt not, be but sworn my love, / And I'll no longer be a Capulet."[5] Unable to remain silent, Romeo emerges from the darkness, and before the night is over they have confessed their love to each other. The momentum set in motion by this chance meeting leads inexorably to catastrophe.

The subject of secrets and love is also important in psychoanalysis, and while it may seem a rather abrupt shift, psychoanalysis is also not irrelevant to the discussion above.

What is particularly interesting here is the phenomenon of transference. Simply put, the concept of transference refers to something in the analysand's personal feelings toward the analyst that is transferred from feelings that once were directed toward people close to the patient. I have brought it into the discussion here because the feelings that constitute transference are those relating to love, or something approaching love. It follows that what I have said above concerning love also applies to transference.

In fact, Freud's conception of transference becomes much easier to understand when it is viewed in this light. Freud considered transference first as an obstacle to analysis, and pointed out that while the analytical situation is no doubt the occasion for transference, analysis itself does not create transference. He then suggested that transference would rarely be spoken of directly by the analysand, and that there was danger of overlooking it if the analyst were not alert to the possibility of its presence. It is clear from this that Freud perceived the fact that the psychology of love that makes its appearance in transference demands a human relationship that is different from the one implied by the conditions of therapy.

So far as the object of therapy is concerned, the patient should feel no hesitation in divulging the pathological part of the psyche to the therapist. This is even more true in psychoanalysis, for it is a prior condition that the analysand reveal things about himself or herself to the analyst freely and without reserve. But transference is precisely what arises in the analysand's heart as a secret he or she wants to hide from the analyst despite this prior condition. Therefore, unless the analyst indicates that he or she is prepared to accept this, deferring the question of therapy itself temporarily, the patient will not reveal it spontaneously. It was Freud's genius, however, that he perceived that the cause of the illness itself was concealed in the transference, and this perception gave birth to a unique theory of transference, and subsequently to the development of transference analysis, one of the most powerful tools of contemporary psychoanalysis.

The subject of secrets and love also suggests new perspectives on *amae*, itself a form of love. The psychology of *amae* is one in which the individual depends on another's love, and feelings of intimacy are in the foreground from the very beginning. From this point of view, it is easy to assume that *amae* is unrelated to the kinds of secrets of love discussed above. In the case of love between parent and child, or between husband and wife, the word love seems to have little connection with secrets. Even in the case of romantic love, once two people have confessed their love for each other and have actually become lovers, they begin to seek indulgent love from each other—that is, they *amaeru*. Generally speaking, it can almost be said that romantic love itself cannot come into existence unless the desire for *amae* (the desire to be indulged) is already secretly present.

Seen in this light, it is possible to conclude that love is a secret only until it is confessed, that once it is confessed, or in a relationship in which it need not be confessed, love is not a secret at all. But this is an extremely superficial way of looking at love. Certainly, for lovers, the fact that they are in love is no secret. But love itself always implies something that is secret.

There are important ways in which *amae* is related to secrets. Consider the case of a person who appears to the outside observer to be displaying *amae* behavior, but is not consciously aware of it. There are even cases in which such a person feels frustrated or dissatisfied at not being permitted to *amaeru*, even though it is clear to the observer that he or she is doing precisely that. Conversely, a person may appear not to be displaying *amae* behavior when internally his or her heart is full of *amae* feelings. *Amae* itself is an emotion that is constituted tacitly. It is telepathic, pre-linguistic, and does not need the medium of language. It is communicated directly from heart to heart. Certainly, it is an emotion of intimacy, but it is also fundamentally related to secrets of the heart.

The analysis above is based on the results of my psychoanalytical research, and much of it is covered in *The Anatomy of Dependence*. I have referred to *amae* in this context because I want to emphasize that *amae*, as a form of love, is no exception to the truth that love is secret. There are aspects of this analysis that are somewhat contradictory. For the person who is displaying *amae* behavior but is unaware of it, *amae* is not so much a secret as a secret turned on its head. That is, while everyone around the person knows that that person's behavior is *amae*, the person himself or herself does not. Perhaps it is possible to describe this by saying that the secret of *amae*, which should belong to that person, has become a secret that betrays the person.

This condition corresponds to the case we considered in Chapter Seven of a person who is unable to have his or her own secrets and whose psyche is ill as a consequence. This condition arises precisely because secrecy is absent. By its very nature, *amae* must be accepted in silence. Therefore, for the satisfaction of *amae*, secrecy is indispensable. Because secrecy is missing, the desire for *amae* is not satisfied, and a sickness of the heart, which is a disruption of the individual's feelings of love in life, is the result.

I would like to conclude this chapter by returning to Hans Asmussen's book, *The Secret of Love*. Asmussen observes that while conversations between a mother and her child, or between two lovers, may sound silly to the outside observer, they have an inexhaustible abundance of meaning for the people intimately involved in them. Based on this observation, he concludes, "Hence, it follows that love is secret, and that it must be secret." He states further that "the beauty of love depends on its secrecy. There is also beauty that is public. But the profoundest beauty is secret. . . . Thus our hearts are corrupt when secrets are missing. This is especially true in love, for love bares the human heart." And what this means for Asmussen is that, "in love, human beings bare the deepest places of the heart," and, therefore, "when love begins, secrecy must envelop both lovers. If it does not, human beings disintegrate."[6]

Based on this point of view, Asmussen warns that the noise of contemporary popular music threatens to cheapen the emotion of love. Furthermore, because "it pertains to the grandeur of the human being that its innermost recesses are revealed in the body," clothing should not be worn merely to protect us from the wind and rain, but should also protect our interiority from the gazes of others.[7] Finally, he laments that the most characteristic aspect of the modern age is that even while we hurry to strip anything and everything naked—to make everything that was once secret public—it has become increasingly rare for people to truly open their hearts.

Notes

1. Hans Asmussen, *Das Geheimnis der Liebe* (Berlin: Verlag Die Spur, 1964).

2. *Kokoro*, 154.

3. Matt., 6:39.

4. John, 15:13.

5. *Romeo and Juliet*, act 2, scene 2, lines 33–36.

6. Asmussen, 7–10. [Translations from the German by Professor Doi.—Trans.]

7. Ibid., 10.

Conclusion

Does the Story Go On?

I was wondering how to conclude this book when I remembered a lecture given by Saul Bellow in Tokyo when he came to Japan at the invitation of the Japan Foundation.[1] In his discussion of the modern novel after James Joyce, Bellow, himself a Nobel-prize-winning writer, argued that the novel can no longer have a story in the twentieth century, that it can no longer hold out against the turmoil of information that assails our consciousness. Society and politics have the all important stories now, and they make the individual unimportant. If there is a story, we read it. We feel suspense, wondering what will happen next, and we are surprised when something does happen. We believe in the values that lie in the background of the story, values which give meaning to individual lives. But if there is no story, we no longer feel that life has meaning. This is proof of despair: We know what is going to happen, we have seen it all before. And not to have a story is not to have hope.

Bellow's arguments concerning the modern novel are also brilliant observations of the modern spirit. Diversity and super-multitudinousness, despair, a recognition of the limitations of being are all a part of modern life. But Bellow was not arguing that it is no longer possible to tell a story. He was challenging this modern consciousness. And Bellow himself has staked his life as a novelist on the hope that it is possible to tell a story. Listening again to a tape of his lecture, it occurred to me that however much despair seems to dominate contemporary life, it cannot have made its first appearance in the modern age. Despair must have existed in every age.

Sophocles's *Oedipus the King*, which was produced soon after 430 B.C., can be read as a tragedy of despair. Although it has been almost universally regarded as the classic example of a "tragedy of fate," it is much more convincing to see it as a tragedy in which despair manifests itself at the moment the characters in the drama begin anticipating their own fates.[2] This becomes clear in the development of the play itself.

Oedipus sends a messenger to the oracle of Apollo in Delphi to learn what he must do to save Thebes from a terrible plague. The oracle replies that Oedipus must banish or kill the man who murdered Laius, the previous ruler of the city. Oedipus summons the blind prophet Terisias, who is said to know the murderer's identity, and forces him to reveal his knowledge, not realizing that Terisias had refused initially because he knew that Oedipus himself had killed Laius. In disbelief and anger, Oedipus suspects a plot to drive him from the throne, but he learns from Jocasta, his queen, that she had borne a son to Laius, and messengers from Corinth, his birthplace, confirm that Oedipus was that son. He learns the secret of his birth. He was the one who had killed Laius. He had been Laius's abandoned child. And Jocasta, his wife, is also his mother. This horrible accident is the very result of two attempts to anticipate fate.

Before Oedipus was born, an oracle had warned Laius that he would be killed by his own son. He had had Oedipus abandoned in the mountains with the intention of killing him. This is the first attempt to anticipate fate. The second occurs when Oedipus, raised as the son of the King of Corinth, hears a rumor that he is not the king's true son and sets out for Delphi to confirm his true identity. Told by the oracle that he is fated to kill his own father, he flees, determined not to return to Corinth. But as he wanders aimlessly, he is challenged by a group of men on the road. They fight, and he kills them all. The leader of this group was Laius.

It is of course possible to read this play as a tragedy depicting the hopeless struggle of human beings against fate. But it is also possible to say that the tragedy occurs precisely because the human beings in the play think they can anticipate fate. For me, this reading is much closer to reality. Oedipus would never have been abandoned by his father had there not been an oracle that the son would grow up to kill his father, or if Laius had not believed the oracle. Both men's fates would have been much different. Similarly, Oedipus sought the oracle of Delphi himself, and then tried to evade the destiny it portended. Had he not heard the oracle, or if he had not believed it, he would have become the king of Corinth. He would not have been on the road when Laius passed, and he would not have killed him.

As we have seen, what sets Oedipus's tragedy in motion is that he thinks he can see what is going to happen—that he knows how the story will end. This desire to see into the future is almost always an omen of despair. When human beings have hope for the future, they have no desire to know the end of the story. The real meaning of hope is that even while we do not really know what is going to happen, we feel that things somehow will turn out right. Even if things are bad at the moment, they are bound to get better. When people feel that they have to see into the future, they can never see anything in it but disaster. And when they attempt to evade disaster, to escape from despair, they actually invite disaster. Despair becomes harder and harder to bear. This, I think, is the meaning of *Oedipus the King*. And I wonder if Oedipus's despair was not pervasive in ancient times. With the end of the ancient age, the mood of despair retreated from the forefront, leading to a spirit of hope that became the basis for the creation of a magnificent civilization.

Today, despair has once again become the dominant mood. In a world split apart, nuclear war threatens to destroy the human race. People are genuinely frightened, and there is a rising public clamor for a social order that can guarantee a lasting peace. But like *Oedipus the King*, this script has no exit. Lest I be misunderstood, I am not saying that international politics is meaningless, or that it is meaningless to plan for the future. Nor am I foolish enough to deny the very real threat of nuclear war. But this threat can become a debilitating obsession, and this is the problem I want to address here. The quest for peace should be full of hope, but despair has become the spirit of our age, an invisible despair that has taken command of people's consciousness. There is something insane about the present. The same things are repeated over and over again. Only technology advances, while the story of humanity has come to a complete stop.

I believe that the cause of this is the fact that some time in the modern age humanity suddenly began trying to look into the future and that somewhere along the line we began to suffer from the delusion that this is actually possible. Now, instead of placing our hopes in the future, we are trying to predict the future and control it.

This reminds me of the long soliloquy at the beginning of Goethe's *Faust*. Faust cries out in bitter anguish against the limitations of humanity and turns to Nostradamus's book hoping to discover the innermost secrets of the world in necromancy:

> Was it a god who made this mystic scroll,
> To touch my spirit's tumult with its healing,
> And bring the secret world before my soul,
> The hidden drive of Nature's force revealing?

Myself a god?—With lightened vision's leap
I read the riddle of the symbols, hear
The looms of Nature's might that never sleep,
And know at last things spoken of the seer:[3]

But he does not know. He succeeds in summoning the Spirit of the Earth, but the Spirit rejects him. He has mastered every conceivable branch of learning, but he has failed completely to ascend to the world of god and "know how spirit doth speak to spirit." But when one attempts to penetrate the innermost secret of things, to know the *ura* of *ura*, one can only expect despair. Because only despair is possible. In this, Faust anticipates the modern age. And if humanity, or even a single individual, wishes to escape once more from despair, the answer is not to follow Faust and sell our souls to the Devil, but simply to stop trying to second-guess the future. We must begin by recognizing that secrets are at the core of existence. It is only when we do not know the *ura*, when we cannot see what is going to happen next, that our story can begin.

I concluded both of my previous books by suggesting that the future is unpredictable. In *The Psychological World of Natsume Sōseki*, I stated that the very fact that Sōseki's sudden death left his last novel, *Meian*, unfinished may in fact have anticipated the ending of the novel and its ultimate theme: that the illusion of modern man can only be shattered by confronting the reality of death.[4] In the conclusion to *The Anatomy of Dependence*, I spoke of a modern phenomenon of regression, of a uniform tendency toward *amae* behavior, and stated that "no one can say whether this regressive phenomenon in mankind is a mortal sickness or a prelude to a new burst of good health."[5]

I would like to end this book by saying that, while I cannot see the future, I have hope that there is one. I believe our story will continue—beyond our individual deaths, and, yes, even beyond the destruction of this planet by nuclear war or some cosmic accident that we have never even imagined.

Notes

1. Saul Bellow, "Who's Got the Story?—The Novel Since James Joyce," in *Eichōsha Tape Lectures*, (Tokyo: Eichōsha Education Industry, 1972). *"Sutōri wa dare no mono ka?—Jeimuzu Joisu igo no shōsetsu,"* *Kaihō— Kokusai Bunka Kaikan*, no. 29, (Tokyo: International House of Japan, 1972), 1–16.

2. For an interpretation of the play similar to the one here, see Bernard Knox, *"Oedipus the King*: Introduction," in *Sophocles: The Three Theban Plays*, Robert Fagles, trans. (Middlesex: Penguin Books, 1982), 131–153.

3. Johann Wolfgang Goethe, *Faust*, Philip Wayne, trans. (Middlesex: Penguin Books, 1985), 45.

4. Doi Takeo, *The Psychological World of Natsume Sōseki*, William J. Tyler, trans. (Cambridge: Harvard University Press, 1976), 153–154.

5. Doi Takeo, *The Anatomy of Dependence*, John Bester, trans. (Tokyo: Kodansha International, 1985), 165.

APPENDIX ONE

The Psychological Background of the Japanese Experience
of Nature: The Perspective of *Omote* and *Ura*

It is generally agreed that the Japanese experience of nature is
one of communion, of exchange characterized by a subtle intimacy. It is an experience of identification with nature. Much
has been written about this experience both in Japanese and in
other languages, and there is little need to give specific examples here. Instead, what I would like to do in this essay is
consider why this kind of experience seems to be uniquely
Japanese.

Many writers have attributed this experience to Japan's rich
natural environment. The Japanese archipelago stretches from
north to south like an arc along the edge of the Asian continent.
Its mild climate is rich in variation, and each season has its own
unique charm. Watsuji Tetsurō, one of Japan's profoundest
ethical thinkers, emphasized this point in his *Fūdo: Ningengaku-teki Kōsatsu* (Natural Environment: An Anthropological Study).[1] Karaki Junzō, in his recent *Nihonjin no Kokoro no
Rekishi* (A History of the Japanese Heart) focuses on the uniquely Japanese awareness of the passing seasons.[2]

A different approach attempts to explain the unique character of the Japanese experience of nature by pointing to the
fact that Japan does not have a Christian tradition. In the Christian world view, God is the fountainhead of all existence.

Nature may be a comfort for human beings, or even a companion, but it can never give human beings salvation. Human beings seek God and attempt to find peace in God. Even nature shares the anguish of humanity and awaits the salvation of God. In Japan, God, as a creator, is absent, and, therefore, human beings seek comfort by attempting to immerse themselves completely in nature.

There is much to support this view. One may point, for example, to the emergence of the Romantic movement in the eighteenth century, when the influence of Christianity had begun to wane in the West. The tendency of the Romantics to immerse themselves in nature produced results that are very similar to the Japanese experience of nature. But while they are similar, the long Christian tradition still had its influence, and even the Romantics were never able to give themselves up completely to nature. Somewhere in their work, there remains an ego that is opposed to nature. Here is an example from Goethe's poetry:

Wanderers Nachtlied II

Über allen Gipfeln
Ist Ruh,
In allen Wipfeln
Spürest du
Kaum einen Hauch:
Die Vögelein schweigen im Walde.
Warte nur! Balde
Ruhest du auch.

Wayfarer's Night Song II

Over the hilltops all
Is still,
Hardly a breath
Seems to ruffle

Any tree crest;
In the wood not one small bird's song.
Only wait, before long
You too will rest.[3]

In both the original German and Michael Hamburger's English translation, the last two lines of this poem are clearly opposed to the first six lines, creating what is almost a disharmony. Interestingly enough, in the translation of this poem by Ōyama Teiichi, the famous Japanese scholar of German literature, the concluding lines read much differently. Translated literally into English, they would go something like this: How moving. O! / I too would rest.[4] For a Japanese Ōyama's translation evokes a response that is much the same as our response to a haiku by Bashō. It has a completely different feeling from that of the original German. Ōyama has written of the difficulty he faced when he attempted to translate the poem in a manner that would appeal to Japanese sensibilities, and, whether his alteration of the original is justified or not, his explanation is extremely interesting:

> In the end, even Goethe, who is said to have entered into the bosom of nature most profoundly, set the ego and nature in opposition, a fact which leaves us feeling inexplicably ill at ease.[5]

It is certainly true that Japanese are able to enter into nature without complaint. And it is equally true that this is related both to the fact that we are blessed with a natural environment that is sympathetic to human beings and to the fact that the Japanese tradition did not receive the influence of Christianity. However, I find it very difficult to believe that these two factors are enough to explain the phenomenon of a uniquely Japanese experience of nature. I cannot help believing that there must also be some psychological factor that drives the Japanese to seek nature. In other words, I wonder if the Japanese do not in many cases attempt to immerse themselves in nature in order to turn their faces away from the world of human beings, to escape from the pain that is always present in that world.

Recently, at the National Conference on Mental Health (Japan), I chaired a symposium on the Japanese heart (*Nihonjin no kokoro*). The poet Yasunaga Michiko told an interesting story about the *Manyōshū* poet Nukata no Ōkimi. Among her famous nature poems is the following *waka*:

> Waiting for the moon
> About to board our boat
> At the Bay of Nigitazu
> The tide is perfect now
> Let us be away oarsmen.[6]

According to Yasunaga, however, Nukata no Ōkimi composed this poem just after suffering the wrenching emotional experience of witnessing another woman give birth to a child fathered by her beloved husband. But there is not a hint of this in the poem. Her feelings are completely buried in the natural scene. The Japanese have depended on nature in this way since ancient times, seeking to become one with nature whenever something happens in the human world. And it is by doing so that the real heart (*kokoro*) of a Japanese is born.

I think Yasunaga's anecdote supports the reasoning outlined above. Perhaps it can be said that Japanese seek oblivion in nature because complications in human relations operate as a motivating force.

Of course the Japanese have no monopoly on complications in human relations. In a certain sense, Westerners would seem to have more violent disruptions in human relations. Certainly they are more outspoken about conflicts. In fact, in the case of the Japanese, it is almost uncanny how dissension does not appear on the surface (*omote*) even when it exists. Somehow, the surface is glossed over, and to that extent conflicts are hidden in the shadows and often assume an aspect of damp gloom.

But I wonder if this way of dealing with conflicts in human relations is not related to the Japanese love of nature. It may be more accurate to say that Japanese turn to nature because there is something unsatisfying in the way they deal with human relations, rather than to say simply that they escape to nature from human complications. Only this would explain why the Japanese feel able to breathe again when they confront nature, and why, strangely enough, they recover a *kokoro* that is much more human than the *kokoro* they have when they relate to other human beings. If it were only escape, Yasunaga's "birth of a true heart" could not occur.

Against this background, let us reconsider the unique manner in which Japanese deal with human conflict. As I suggested above, the surface is always glossed over, and conflict is shut up in the shadows. Japanese refer to this as *omote* and *ura*. Generally, we use these words unconsciously, but considering the fact that we use them all the time, in all kind of situations, it is unmistakable that they are extremely important concepts in determining the structure of the Japanese consciousness. For example, *omote o tsukurou* means "to keep up appearances." "To attack from the rear" is *ura o kaku*. The saying "in every *ura* there is an *ura*" (*ura ni wa ura ga aru*) suggests the fact that there is a quality of duality in these concepts. It is possible in Japanese to construct a number of contrastive sets based on this dyadic quality: *omote-muki* ("that which is public, open, official") opposed to *ura-muki* ("that which is private, closed, personal"), for instance. In principle, Japanese homes should have two reception halls. The one inside the front door, the *omote-genkan* is for receiving guests. The *ura-genkan* in the rear of the house is for receiving things delivered by the greengrocer, or used by servants. An *omote-dōri* is a busy main street; an *ura-dōri* is a lonely back alley.

Japanese often speak of *tatemae* and *honne*, and there is no better way to express their essence than to say that *tatemae* refers to *omote* while *honne* refers to *ura*. It is also interesting to note that many words used to refer to mental states in classical Japanese contain the word *ura*. *Uraganishi* and *urasabishi* make it explicit that the speaking subject's heart is "sad" or "lonely." *Urayamu* ("to be sick in the heart") means "to envy." To "bear resentment" is to *uramu*. In all these words, *ura* originally signified the same thing as the *ura* of *omote* and *ura*. It is the heart as it is present in *ura* (*ura no kokoro*), the heart that is concealed in *ura* and the heart that never appears in *omote*.

I would like to consider next how Japanese distinguish between *omote* and *ura*. While the distinction is quite clear, it is important to note that they are in a symbiotic, mutually constituting relationship. Without one the other cannot exist. *Ura* performs *omote*, but *omote* is also indispensable. Unless one constructs an *omote*, *ura* cannot be protected. And this is exactly what we mean when we say that *omote* and *ura* form a single entity. Having said that, however, it is indeed strange that it does not matter if they appear from the outside to contradict each other. When one's standpoint is that of *omote*, *omote* is everything. It is as if *ura* does not exist, and it can be ignored. The same can be said of *ura*. Moreover, a Japanese can move adroitly from one standpoint to the other, so adroitly in fact that we are not sure which is *omote* and which is *ura*. The distinction, however, never disappears.

Put in this way, it may sound as if every Japanese is a split personality, but it is precisely this distinction between *omote* and *ura* that has enabled the Japanese to handle ambivalence. The urge to eliminate ambivalence for a higher integrity is generally weak among the Japanese. The average Japanese attempts to get through life by keeping the contradictions between *omote* and *ura* to a minimum and to avoid showing his or her *ura* to others. It is inevitable that a certain amount of dirt will get out. As we often say, if you beat them with a stick, a certain amount of dust will rise from anyone. But if there is an excess, a person will be hated as one who "has an *ura-omote*."

In the process of explaining *omote* and *ura*, I have touched on some of the less redeeming aspects of the Japanese, but it is important to note that this distinction does not always have bad results, for Japanese are able to acquire a true inner life only when they have awakened to it. As stated above, the word *ura* itself refers to the unseen heart, to a *kokoro* that is concealed. And the fact that Japanese distinguish between *omote* and *ura* does not have the purpose of deliberately deceiving others. That is the exception.

To say that a person's nature "does not have *ura-omote*" is an expression of admiration, and it is clear from this that we feel a certain pain when we have to use *omote* and *ura*. In other words, it is not so much that the Japanese like using *omote* and *ura* as that they are forced to become aware of it. One may well ask why this is true. Why must the Japanese make this distinction?

I think this is closely related to the psychology of *amae*, in which I have been interested for some time. Japanese see human relations completely as a function of *amae*.[7] The highest ideal is to be allowed to *amaeru*, and Japanese struggle constantly to approach that ideal. The Japanese love to speak of providing for people's *wa* (harmony), which is an expression of the ideal. But it is extremely difficult to achieve *wa*. It is difficult enough between two people; it is virtually impossible when there is a large group. Still, it is imperative to do something to create an atmosphere of *wa*, and so we set up general principles and, under the supreme command of *wa*, agree on them as the public *omote*. In fact, this is the true form of *tatemae*.

But this by no means prevents the individual from having *honne* in the *ura* of *tatemae*. Indeed, it is perhaps more accurate to say that people should have *honne* at such times. Somehow, *tatemae* is not enough. *Tatemae* is only a sign protecting the *wa* of the group.

This does not mean that *tatemae* is taken lightly. The Japanese place much value on signs. Foreigners often remark that the Japanese are fond of ceremony. Whether the criticism implied by this is justified or not, the observation is not mistaken. But the Japanese know that *omote* forms are essential to the harmonious social life that is the ideal. However, there remains the concealed heart, the *kokoro* in the *ura*, which cannot be satisfied with this, and we are aware of this as our *honne*. In this way, it can be said that the Japanese distinguish between *omote* and *ura* because of the psychology of *amae*, which in the unconscious rules their psychic lives.

This is also clear from the fact that the distinction between *omote* and *ura* corresponds to the dyadic concepts of *uchi* and *soto*, which Japanese use when they divide types of human relations depending on the degree of tolerance of *amae* behavior. The Japanese show only *omote* when they deal with relationships of obligation (*giri*) in the outside (*soto*). But in intimate, unreserved relationships of *uchi*, they reveal *ura*. *Soto* is *omote* and *uchi* is *ura*, and so the words are also consistent, *uchi* and *soto* referring to a dual structure of human relations, while *ura* and *omote* refer to the existence of a dual structure of consciousness. In fact, a Japanese is not considered to be an adult until he has become aware of these distinctions.

Therefore, when there are some impediments or disturbances in mental development, as is the case with psychosis or neurosis, we see confusion in the distinction between *omote* and *ura*. This occurs in many forms. Some people have never been able to make the distinction. In other cases, the patient somehow has made a distinction, but is constantly troubled because his or her *ura* reveals itself in *omote* situations. Some patients understand the distinction, but cannot effectively use *omote* and *ura*. Sometimes *omote* becomes merely a kind of sign, advertising one thing while the person is in fact quite different. Among the most tragic cases are those in which a patient has completely lost sight of his or her own *ura*.

I suggested earlier that the Japanese love of nature is due to the fact that there is something unsatisfying about the way we deal with human conflict. As we have seen, Japanese do so by making a distinction between *omote* and *ura*. Perhaps it is true that this is unavoidable, perhaps we cannot hope for healthy mental development without this distinction. But it is also impossible to deny that learning to do so is accompanied by a kind of pain, because the distinction between *omote* and *ura* implies a splitting of consciousness. We have to do something with the *kokoro* that exists in *ura*, which is not revealed to the outside (*omote*). It is quite convenient to make the distinction, but it is also exhausting. I believe that the Japanese turn to nature for healing when their hearts are split, when they weary of this splitting of consciousness. Nature does not have an *omote* and an *ura*. Therefore, it can be trusted completely. Only when the Japanese can touch nature can they experience a "true heart."

Japanese sometimes have feelings of superiority toward Westerners, who in their eyes cannot easily become one with nature. The Japanese never experience the splitting of the body and the soul that occurs in the consciousness of Western people. And they are not afflicted by the Christian conflict between spirit and flesh, nor burdened by the severe dichotomy of subject and object that is inherent in the Western philosophical tradition. This may be true. But the Japanese are afflicted, nevertheless, with the splitting of the consciousness into *omote* and *ura*, and we must not forget the fact that we seek to become one with nature precisely because of this affliction.

Notes

1. Watsuji Tetsurō, *Fūdo: Ningengaku-teki Kōsatsu* [Natural Environment: An Anthropological Study] (Tokyo: Chikuma Shobō, 1935). For a complete translation in English, see Watsuji Tetsurō, *Climate and Culture*, Jeffrey Bownas, trans. (Tokyo: Hokuseidō, 1971).

2. Karaki Junzō, *Nihonjin no Kokoro no Rekishi* [History of the Japanese Heart] (Tokyo: Chikuma Shobō, 1970).

3. Johann Wolfgang Von Goethe, in *Goethe: Poems and Epigrams*: Selected, Translated and with an Introduction by Michael Hamburger (London: The Anvil Press, 1983), 25.

4. Ōyama Teiichi, *Gette* [Goethe], *Sekai Koten Bungaku Zenshū* [Compendium of World Classics] (Tokyo: Chikuma Shobō, 1985).

5. Cited in Herrmann Heuvers, *Ningen wa tsukurareta mono: Bungaku ni arawareta sei-kanjō* [What Man Has Wrought: Feelings of Life As They Have Appeared in Literature], *Seiki* [Century (magazine)], April, 1957.

6. *Manyōshū* [The Ten Thousand Leaves], poem 8.

7. For a detailed discussion of *amae*, see Doi Takeo, *The Anatomy of Dependence*, John Bester, trans. (Tokyo and New York: Kodansha International, 1985).

APPENDIX TWO

Omote and *Ura*: Concepts Derived from the Japanese
2-Fold Structure of Consciousness

Bill Caudill and I met for the first time in 1954, when he was having his first Japanese experiences and I was groping to formulate my clinical experiences in terms of what I learned in America. Subsequent years made us real comrades in arms, since I served as a consultant to his research in Japan and he was a most appreciative audience as I was developing my own thinking. I was much encouraged because he so often cited my work in his papers and I wrote many papers in English thanks to his support. We even produced one joint paper, "Interrelations of Psychiatry, Culture and Emotion in Japan"[1], which summarized some of our congruent viewpoints and findings. What follows now has been written as an extension of our long collaborative work. I think Bill would have approved of my saying this with his characteristic understanding smile.

Let me first explain the title of this paper, for the readers may wonder at once what is so unique about the 2-fold or even multifold structure of consciousness. Doesn't everyone have some things that he wants to keep to himself or to confide only to someone very close? The front he presents to the public eye is often different from what he thinks he is. According to William James, "A man has as many social selves as there are individuals who recognize him and carry an image of him in their

157

mind."[2] All this is certainly true, and I acknowledge that what I call the Japanese 2-fold structure of consciousness is essentially a universal human trait. Only I want to say that this trait is cultivated to an unusual extent in Japan so that it has come to represent a definite pattern of living. Hence, the need to use special concepts to describe it.

These concepts are conveyed by two Japanese words, *omote* and *ura*, which Japanese use to indicate the contrasting attitudes in dealing with social situations. These words, like the English equivalents "front" and "rear," literally refer to the fore and back sides of things. Apart from this literal use, however, they are sometimes used in naming things to suggest the social function of the thing thus named. For instance, *omote-guchi* (front door) is the main entrance to Japanese houses which is of use for the members of a family or their guests, but the maid or the shopmen who call either to take orders or to deliver things use only *ura-guchi* (kitchen-door). *Omote-dōri* or *omote-kaidō* is a busy street and *ura-dōri* or *ura-kaidō* a lonely alley, hence these two words may be used to imply a success or the lack of it. As can be seen from these usages, *omote* is the appearance one would show to others. In this respect it is interesting to note that *omote* means "face" and *ura* "mind" in old literary Japanese. That one is able to build up *omote* is a commendable thing in Japan. It means that one is finally on one's own. It is different from a similar English expression, "to put up a front," which has the bad connotation of making a show. *Ura* is the reverse of *omote*, that is, what one would hide from others. Hence, to take *ura* (*ura o kaku*) is to attack from behind. To cut *ura* (*uragiru*) is to betray. That *ura* aches (*urayamu*) is to envy. It is also used as prefix to some adjectives, such as *ura-ganashii* (sad), *ura-sabishii* (lonely), to indicate that one who so feels cannot identify its cause.

Thus, when Japanese say the affairs of *omote* (*omote no hanashi*), they mean what they do in order to impress others whose presence puts them on guard. Conversely, when they say the matters of *ura* (*ura no hanashi*), they mean their secrets which they will disclose only to those who are closest to them. These two might contradict each other in substance, but that doesn't matter to Japanese. Furthermore, when one is in the state of *omote*, *omote* is everything and *ura* virtually does not exist for him. Likewise, when one is in *ura*, one can forget about the existence of *omote*. Only one should be able to discern which is the time for *omote* and which for *ura*. The ease with which one shifts from *omote* to *ura* and back again without much strain is regarded as the measure of one's social maturity. In other words, it doesn't blemish a man's integrity to take recourse to one or the other depending upon the particular situation he finds himself in. Rather his integrity rests upon the complete mastery of *omote* and *ura*.

In this connection I would like to introduce two more Japanese words, *tatemae* and *honne*. *Tatemae* is a certain formal principle which is palatable to everybody concerned so that the harmony of a group is guaranteed, while *honne* is the feelings or opinions which they privately hold regarding the matter. It is admitted that there may be an apparent discrepancy between the two, yet they are supposed to coexist in peace. It must be clear from this explanation that the relationship of *tatemae* to *honne* is the same as that of *omote* to *ura*. As a matter of fact, *tatemae* and *honne* can perhaps best be defined as the *omote*-mind and the *ura*-mind respectively. Japanese evidently need both. The two are complementary to each other. Literally there is no *omote* (front) without *ura* (rear) and no *ura* without *omote*. Likewise, *tatemae* doesn't stand alone without tacit support from *honne* and the latter cannot be entertained without the former's protection.

Why do Japanese make much of the distinction between *omote* and *ura*, that is, the distinction between what can be shown to others and what cannot and elevate it to a rule of daily living? I think this is definitely related to the psychology of *amae* that prevails in Japanese society, which I explained in a number of articles.[3] *Amae* is a dependency need which manifests itself in a longing to merge with others. This longing can be fulfilled under satisfactory conditions in infancy, but surely it cannot be easily fulfilled as one grows up. But if *amae* is set forth as the principle of a society regulating the smooth transactions of its members, wouldn't that society have to institute a certain token indicating that this need is taken care of? I think that is what happened in Japanese society. Namely, *omote* or *tatemae* is a token that the mutuality of members of a group is preserved, while *ura* or *honne* which acknowledges the inevitable frustrations in *amae* is given free rein as long as it does not dispute the former. This is surely a very ingenious way of handling ambivalent feelings. The fact that Japanese frequently exchange gifts saying, "This is only an *oshirushi* (token) of my gratitude (or apology)," is definitely related to this. It also explains why Japanese look so homogeneous and cohesive, yet if and when no *tatemae* is available why they so easily resort to violence.

The above description of the Japanese 2-fold structure of consciousness might give an impression that it is after all a double standard of morality. This impression is perhaps strongest among foreigners who have to make a certain deal with Japanese. They of course do not share the same values with Japanese. What Japanese present to them as *omote* or *tatemae* sounds to them like empty words. So they complain that Japanese are shrewd and vain in spite of their apparent politeness and sincerity, that Japanese are too fond of formalities even in social intercourse and seldom reveal what they really think and feel. I should maintain, however, that Japanese do not espouse the double standard of morality deliberately. Rather it is truer to say that they are driven toward it because of their cultural heritage, as I explained above. Furthermore, at times Japanese themselves may find it unhappy to behave in *omote* or *ura* alternately. In fact, to learn how to do it is a growing pain for every Japanese child. For many adults the pain they incurred as a child ensues in the permanent splitting of their ego. They cannot integrate *omote* and *ura* adequately. Hence, they envy and extol a person who appears to have no splitting of *omote* and *ura* and hate intensely anybody who makes use of such splitting to promote his selfish interest.

I think that the famous Japanese fondness of nature can also be understood from the same angle. For Japanese must feel greatly relieved with nature since they don't have to play *omote* and *ura* with it. They become one with nature so to speak and can indulge in the feeling of pure *amae*. From their viewpoint therefore they feel more human with nature than with humans. Lest it be thought, however, that I maintain that such an attitude toward nature is only peculiarly Japanese, let me quote a few lines from William Wordsworth's *Tintern Abbey Revisited*, which seem to echo exactly the same feelings:

> ". . . well pleased to recognize
> In Nature and the language of the sense,
> The anchor of my purest thoughts, the nurse,
> The Guide, the guardian of my heart, and soul
> Of all my moral being . . .
> Knowing that Nature never did betray
> The heart that loved her."

So such fond feelings for nature are not exclusively Japanese, though it may be said that they are much more pronounced and pervasive in Japan. In fact Japan had not just one Wordsworth, but hundreds and thousands like him who gave expression to those feelings. One would argue further that even Wordsworth was too discursive compared with the total immersion of Japanese in nature. So far so good. But this main relationship

Japanese have with nature has one basic defect: It doesn't teach Japanese how to protect and spare nature. That is, I believe, why they did practically nothing to prevent the vast destruction wrought upon nature in recent years. It could happen in spite of their extreme fondness of nature, or, to put it ironically, perhaps because of it.

Finally, I should like to mention one general usage of the concepts *omote* and *ura*, though they were originally invented to describe the Japanese 2-fold structure of consciousness. I think this is possible because the concepts are sufficiently abstract. The fact that they refer to a very critical period of life when a child begins to distinguish between what he can say to others and what he cannot makes them particularly applicable to psychiatric thinking. For one could assume that without acquiring such a distinction a child would not come to awareness of his inner self and consequently there would be no healthy growth of his ego. Also, as I noted above, if to distinguish between *omote* and *ura* is a way of handling ambivalent feelings, it must be especially worthwhile to investigate how it fares in different psychiatric conditions.

Now what follows is a tentative sketch of my experimenting with these concepts in identifying various types of psychopathology. First, neurotics seem to be those whose *ura* threatens to come out against their better judgment. In other words, they cannot contain *ura* safely within themselves in spite of their capacity to distinguish between *omote* and *ura*. Second, psychopaths seem to be those who think they can get away with *ura*, casting *omote* to the winds. Third, epileptics seem to be those who, though ordinarily holding fast to the distinction between *omote* and *ura*, may suddenly feel compelled to discard such a distinction for a "total" consciousness. Fourth, manic depressives seem to be those who are convinced that they have no *ura*. In other words, they have put all their heart in *omote*. But if a time comes when they can no longer maintain *omote*, *ura* will come out with all its vehemence either in the form of a manic or a depressive state. Fifth, schizophrenics seem to be those who failed to develop the sense of *omote* and *ura* at a proper developmental time. They are transparent to others and to themselves as well. So when they are later forced by external circumstances to distinguish between *omote* and *ura*, they are bound to break down into a confused state.

Thus, it seems possible to characterize various types of psychopathology in terms of *omote* and *ura*. It is simple, neat, and I believe, meaningful even without nosological nomenclature. One could perhaps say that it gives new meanings to the old nosological concepts. It has also the advantage of being able to tie up quite well with a detailed study of psychodynamics. I shall be happy indeed if this proposition is further tested by Western psychiatrists.

[Editor's Note: This article was written by Dr. Doi for a special issue of the *Journal of Nervous and Mental Disease* (157:258–261, 1973) in memory of William Caudill. It is reproduced by permission and contains no changes except for the treatment of footnotes to make them consistent with the rest of the book.]

Notes

1. William Caudill and Doi Takeo, "Interrelations of Psychiatry, Culture, and Emotion in Japan," in *Man's Image in Medicine and Anthropology*, I. Galdstone, ed. (New York: International Universities Press, New York, 1963).

2. William James, *The Principles of Psychology* (New York: Henry Holt and Co., 1890), 294.

3. Doi Takeo, "*Amae*: A Key Concept for Understanding Japanese Personality Structure," in *Japanese Culture: Its Development and Characteristics*, R. J. Smith and R. K. Beardsley, eds. (Aldine, Chicago, 1963); "*Giri-Ninjō*: An Interpretation," in *Aspects of Social Change*, R. P. Dore, ed. (Princeton, New Jersey: Princeton University Press, 1967); "Some Thoughts on Helplessness and the Desire to Be Loved," *Psychiatry*, 1963, 26: 266–272.

INDEX

Acts of Worship Seven Stories

Yukio Mishima/Translated by John Bester

These seven consistently interesting stories, each with its own distinctive atmosphere and mood, are a timely reminder of Mishima the consummate writer.

Sun and Steel

Yukio Mishima/Translated by John Bester

This fascinating document—part autobiography, part reflections on the search for personal identity—traces Mishima's life from an introverted childhood to a creative maturity.

House of Nire

Morio Kita/Translated by Dennis Keene

A comic novel that captures the essence of Japanese society while chronicling the lives of the Nire family and their involvement in the family-run mental hospital.

Stranger in Tibet
The Adventures of a Wandering Zen Monk

Scott Berry

The fascinating biography of a young Zen monk who managed to enter the forbidden city of Lhasa during the turn of the century.